Raven
MY YEAR
OF DATING
dangerously

Monica Porter is a London-based journalist.
She has two sons, and two grandsons, and
has written five books. To find out more,
visit: www.monicaporter.co.uk

Also by

MONICA PORTER

The Paper Bridge:
A Return to Budapest

Deadly Carousel: A Singer's Story
of the Second World War

Dreams and Doorways: Turning Points in the
Early Lives of Famous People

Long Lost: The Story of the Newspaper Column
that Started the Reunion Industry

Raven

MY YEAR OF DATING *dangerously*

MONICA PORTER

306.7092

HEAD
of
ZEUS

First published in the UK in 2014 by Thistle Publishing
This edition published in eBook and paperback in the UK in 2014
by Head of Zeus Ltd.

1 3 5 7 9 10 8 6 4 2

A CIP catalogue record for this book is available
from the British Library.

Paperback ISBN: 9781784081515
eBook ISBN: 9781784081508

Typeset by e-type, Aintree, Liverpool

Printed and bound by CPI Group (UK) Ltd,
Croydon, CR0 4YY

HEAD OF ZEUS LTD
Clerkenwell House
45-47 Clerkenwell Green
London EC1R OHT

WWW.HEADOFZEUS.COM

For Sara, of course

I have been a journalist all my life and on many occasions written about my personal experiences in the field of human relationships. Perhaps it is what I do best. 'The man who writes about himself and his own time is the only man who writes about all people and all time,' was how George Bernard Shaw put it and I believe that to be true...and to apply equally to women.

Having said that, I didn't set out on the adventures described in this book with the primary intention of writing about them. Even if I hadn't had a book in mind – even if I weren't a journalist at all but a pharmacist, say, or a shoe designer – I would have done exactly the same things in the same way. Because in the 21st century, a woman in my situation is almost bound to open the Pandora's box of online dating. It's just that some of us do it with a bit more gusto. And take notes.

As well as the names of all the men included in the book, I have changed some surface details about them (such as their jobs or geographical locations) so that they would be identifiable to no one other than themselves. If I accidently hit upon anyone's actual user-name on a dating site somewhere, my apologies. In two or three cases I created composites of different individuals for, as they say, dramatic purposes. But I didn't invent anything; I didn't need to.

'No animals were harmed in the making of this film,' you will often read as the credits roll at the end of a movie. And I am glad to say that, bruised egos aside, no people were hurt in the making of this book. Not even me, although risks there were aplenty. And ultimately that is what I should like the more starchy and censorious of my critics to bear in mind, so that they can direct their opprobrium at more appropriate targets.

*I*t was July, 2012. I woke up that morning to the realisation that it was my sixtieth birthday. It sounded so much older and scarier than fifty – and I had thought *that* was bad enough. I still felt young (well, pretty young) and forward-looking. There was much I had yet to see and do. But sixty. That was a depressing concept. Would I even still be considered middle-aged or was sixty the irrefutable herald of something a lot worse: the realm of old age, the pension and the bus pass? The whole thing made me shudder and want to pull the duvet over my head. But I stretched, got up and made the coffee.

Three months earlier my partner and I had split up. We had been together for thirteen years. It had become a rickety relationship, for sure, but nevertheless there is something reassuring about having an 'other half', especially if you're an older woman who fears loneliness. I'd never lived entirely alone before. And those past three months had not been easy as sole occupant of the house that once was our shared space, surrounded by memories of happier times as a couple, eating my solitary dinner on a tray in front of the telly. Mine was a home now infused with a sense of loss and failure, it felt hollow and much too quiet.

So there I was, single and sixty and feeling on the scrap heap. It seemed as if it was all over for me – the love and passion, the sex and sensuality. I wondered whether I should just relegate those excitements to my past. After all, I'd had my share. Perhaps from now on I would focus on my relationships with my children and grandchildren. Move into a granny annex, perhaps? Yes, that's it. We can be like the Waltons. Love all round. I'll be the beloved matriarch, sitting by the fire and counting my blessings...

Another morning, four months later. I wake up with a fuzzy head and I'm exhausted. Every muscle aches. But on the inside I'm smiling. I've just spent virtually the whole night indulging in carnal delights with my good-looking new friend, aged twenty-six. Yes (shocking, I admit), he is younger than both my sons but in some miraculous way the yawning age gap made no difference. We had a great time. And best of all, there was nothing sleazy about it. We didn't meet in some pick-up joint or through a kinky advert. We were properly introduced by a mutual friend at a social gathering, started chatting, hit it off, discovered a shared love of classic films and took it from there. And to think I assumed he was only interested in my DVD collection.

Scrap heap? Hardly. As it turned out, I was just cranking up again. Because the truth is that in the great game of intimate human relationships, it ain't over until you stop breathing.

The theme of being an older single woman on the so-called dating scene is of special pertinence to me, as I have found myself occupying this demographic space twice in my lifetime – first in the 1990s, following the breakdown of my marriage, and again now, two decades later. I regard myself as a staunch individualist but have to admit that in this respect I have landed smack in the middle of the social statistics.

When I got divorced at the age of forty after a 17-year marriage which produced two sons, I emerged blinking into the glare of a dating scene radically different to that of my pre-marriage youth. In my new life as a single working mother I had a variety of misadventures with the opposite sex.

As my second long-term relationship ended exactly twenty years later, at sixty (I find this symmetry pleasing in a rather perverse way), I found that the scene had spectacularly moved on yet again, to the internet and array of new technologies and procedures. A bewildering landscape, but I was glad to see how thoroughly accepted, how free of embarrassment and stigma online dating had become by the end of the first decade of the 21st century. It seemed as if pretty much everyone was doing it. So, despite my lingering sense that there was something inherently tawdry about it, I decided to leap off the diving board into that murky water below.

Well-meaning friends offered advice on the requirements for attracting a man, online or otherwise. Maya, my 35-year-old, half-Asian, racy chum (the raciness stemming from the non-Asian half, obviously), told me I should start wearing a push-up bra and red lipstick. 'It works for me,' she said. And my gay friend Tim suggested I colour my hair blonde and get a boob job because 'straight guys go for a big cleavage'. Needless to say, I didn't do any of those things.

To find out what I *did* do, at the coal face of today's daring digital dating scene, read on...

... $\mathcal{B}$ut forgive me if I digress briefly in order to trace the route which brought me to my present state of mature singledom, something I neither wanted nor expected. In some ways it's a classic tale, emblematic of my post-war generation. But in other respects my back story is unconventional.

Although born in Budapest, I spent most of my childhood and adolescence in New York. My Hungarian mother was very strict, so as well as feeling set apart from my peers for cultural reasons, I had to battle against her quasi-Victorian values which kept me from the free-and-easy, all-American lifestyle I longed to embrace. My writer father was somewhat less strict, but focused chiefly on earning a living to support his young immigrant family, so he left the child-rearing to my mother. Unfortunately for me.

As a teenager I had to do a lot of sneaking around in order to spend time with boys. I didn't actually get up to anything beyond smooching and a little light petting, so my mother needn't have worried. But worried she was, the reins were kept tight, and I didn't 'go all the way' (as we used to say in high school) until I was pushing twenty. Then for the next year it was a patchy affair with a small handful of ill-chosen men – and still clandestine, as I was living at home, by now in London.

Small wonder then, that when at the age of twenty-one I met the first 'proper' and respectable prospect – a lawyer, no less – and we hit it off and my parents approved, and the opportunity to slip my reins presented itself, I married him. Within the year.

My husband was seven years older, which made for a paternalistic relationship, but in the heady early days of the marriage this didn't seem to pose a problem. In fact it felt sort of natural to go from my parental home to a household run by a paternalistic husband who was more established than me, earned more money than me, knew more than me. Having had no previous experience of a serious relationship, I had to feel my way around. I was used to kicking against my parents' authority. Could I – should I – kick against his too? I was at the tail end of the generation that still felt, back in the seventies, that it was okay for the man of the house to 'wear the trousers'. So we weren't a partnership of equals. Although if I'd been, like him, in my late twenties when we married, and not twenty-two, this dynamic might not have existed for us even then. The truth was that I was just very green.

There was a telling episode, very early in the marriage, which I sometimes later reflected on, as it foreshadowed the eventual demise of our union. We were giving a party and I was in the bathroom applying mascara and eye-liner. My husband came in, gave me a disapproving glance and told me I didn't need make-up, I looked 'pretty enough' without it. (His mother had never worn eye make-up, and men often look to their mums for the ideal.) Well, I loved my husband, so with a shrug I obligingly removed the make-up.

But a little later, as the party got into full swing and I saw that most of our young women friends – the more attractive ones, at least – were wearing mascara and eye-liner and maybe even the pale blue eye shadow so fashionable at the time, I snuck back to the bathroom and got dolled up again. Defiantly I returned to the shindig in full war paint and when my husband glanced my way I merely grinned at him.

There were some good things about that marriage, not least the production of two fine sons, but the inequality in our relationship, its composition of a 'senior partner' and 'junior partner' became more, not less, pronounced over the years. Not surprisingly, as I developed into my own person, gathering strength and self-assurance along the way, the more that tidy arrangement failed to wash. And of course I eventually escaped my restraints – again! – this time into the embrace of someone who took it as read that we were on a par and knew how to really *listen*. But the marriage later recovered (one doesn't ditch this commitment lightly when young children are involved) and it was many more years before it broke down for good.

I had no idea when I embarked on the life of the divorcee, having just turned forty, what a precipitous learning curve it would be with regard to the male of the species. Not just the startling discovery that 99% of married men – even the ostensibly 'good' ones – are inclined to dabble in extra-marital high-jinks sooner or later, but the full appreciation of how generally roguish men are, whether married or not.

Take Exhibit A: a successful composer, twenty-five years older than me, who became a neighbour when my sons and I moved into a west London flat after the marital split. He took me out on a couple of dates, we went to the cinema and out for dinner and told each other about our lives – the usual sort of thing. He was an interesting, affable fellow and we got on well but I didn't view him as a romantic prospect. You have to be physically attracted to a person for that – at least a little.

On our second date, while having a late-night coffee back at his flat, he took umbrage at my refusal to cuddle up. I asked whether we couldn't simply be friends. (Shades of *When Harry Met Sally*.) He said no, we couldn't; it was to be a sexual relationship or nothing. I was unceremoniously booted out and never heard from him again. Forget neighbourly. He cut me dead whenever we passed on the street.

Exhibit B is the hard-drinking, chain-smoking, cowboy-booted Liverpudlian disc jockey I went out with for nearly a year. He appealed to me mainly because of his novelty value: he was as different from a lawyer as it's humanly possible to be. He would dedicate golden oldies to me on the radio and take me along to broadcasting parties where I met other celebrated DJs. And he could be amusing to have around (that is, before consuming his habitual half-bottle of whisky and lumbering around like a Neanderthal, a fag hanging from his mouth).

But he had a dark side, possibly stemming from his impoverished wartime childhood in bombed-out Bootle. His seaman father deserted the family and it was tough going for him until he found his niche in pirate radio. There was certainly some grim history festering beneath the surface because every so often he would say something obnoxious or throw his weight around. One night he grabbed my nine-year-old son by the lapels and pushed him up against a wall for some perceived misdemeanour, so I told him to leave and knew that he wasn't long for my world.

Which leads us to Exhibit C, a colleague whose persistent advances finally won me over, whereupon I was pleasantly surprised to find I rather liked his company. Everything went well for a while until the evening we had arranged to meet at a pub near our office, popular with many of our work-mates. We met up as planned and ordered our drinks, then chatted amiably to a few others around us. But within half an hour I realised he had honed in on a young blonde sitting at a table with a crowd of friends. He managed to squeeze in beside her and although he had his back to me, his body language was plain enough to read. Having arranged to be at the pub with me, he lost little time in trying to pull someone else. What could I do? I finished my drink and left. And that was the end of that little involvement. It hurt.

Exhibit D: a travel assignment once took me on an ele-phant trek through northern Thailand in the company of a dashing guide, an Englishman in his thirties. We got to know each other intimately as (on one memorable night) we shared a tent in the middle of the eerie jungle. He and his wife had separated; from what he told me she sounded like an abso-lute harridan and he said he was relieved to be out of it. But he missed his young daughter.

We began a relationship and when he returned to England a few weeks later, made plans for a romantic weekend break. I looked forward to our long-awaited reunion with my cus-tomary ardour – the things we would say, the things we would do. But the day before we were due to meet he rang me at the office to say he had gone back to his wife. He explained that he didn't want to do it but for his daughter's sake he had to give the marriage another go. So that was me dumped, again. I spent the rest of the day crying in the ladies' loo.

By now you doubtless get the drift. Single or hitched, young or long in the tooth, men are a slippery lot and you really ought not to depend on them. Don't get me wrong, I'm fond of the bastards – life would be so boring without them – but like feral animals, you pet them at your peril. Few of them actually mean to cause hurt, but again, like those feral beasts they can't help it because it's in their DNA.

I should have learnt that eternal truth long ago, perhaps back in 1992, when I'd just moved out of the marital home and into a place of my own. I spent the first three days unpacking and putting everything into its place, then decided to explore my new neighbourhood. It was a sunny summer's afternoon. After my walk I stopped in at a pleasant café. No empty tables. But there was a table with a lone man sitting at it, and he was very handsome with his dark hair and moustache so I decided that that was the table for me. I asked him whether I could sit down, he said yes of course and I ordered a coffee. Then I asked if I might read a part of his newspaper, as I hadn't seen a paper for days.

'Oh, have you been travelling?' he inquired.

'No, just moved into the area. Been busy unpacking.'

And so it began. We talked and talked, ordered more coffees, then talked some more. Instant rapport. And a mounting mutual attraction which almost made the air crackle. He was a barrister, a bachelor aged 38 – two years younger than me. We sat together in the café until the other customers had all left and the staff started closing up for the day. He escorted me home, came up to my flat to fix a plug onto my new iron because I am no good at that sort of thing, then as we were standing at the door saying good-bye he unexpectedly invited me out to dinner that evening.

Two hours later we were enjoying a candlelit meal over a bottle of wine at a quiet local restaurant, it was all getting deliciously romantic, and I began to feel as if I were in a dream. Not only good-looking and easy to talk to, he was also warm and thoughtful and sensitive. Had I really just left my marriage and walked straight into the love affair from heaven? *In three days?*

Things got even better afterwards back at my place. Suffice it to say that during a long and rapturous night he fulfilled all expectations, and then some. I was smitten.

We saw each other every weekend for a number of weeks and it was wonderful. He introduced me to his best friend and his best friend's girlfriend and the four of us double-dated. We chatted about all going sailing together down on the south coast, where the two men kept a boat. 'You know how to hoist a mainsail, don't you?' he asked me. '*No?* Then you can lie around in a bikini and be decorative!' Laughs all round.

Perhaps you can guess where I'm going with this, and it isn't heavenwards.

One night at his trendy bachelor pad I sensed a slight cooling, and after that he suddenly disappeared. He didn't call, or return my calls. Well, he did eventually, but it was only to tell me that we couldn't be together any more, which gave me that instant painful stab in the pit of the stomach familiar to every 'dumpee'. I had to persuade him to meet me at a local pub in order to explain his motives.

This was his speech: 'This is really hard for me because I'm going to say something that I know will hurt you.' Pause. 'There's somebody else.' Another pause, as he stared down at his drink. 'You see, you've already been married and had your children, but I haven't done any of that yet and it's something I want to do. I need someone who wants to start a family with me. And I think I may have found her…at last.'

That I'd been married, had children, was forty and therefore maybe not the ideal yummy-mummy candidate were all things he knew about me before we had finished our second cup of coffee on the day we met. So if it was kids he was after, what had been the whole point of our steamy relationship? At that moment, sitting in the pub, it seemed as if its sole purpose had been to land me in an ocean of pain.

The moral of the story is this: if someone so wonderful, so warm, thoughtful and sensitive – and he genuinely *was* all those things – could dump you in the shit, what about the lesser men, the unthinking and insensitive specimens? What in god's name were *they* capable of?

By the time I met my partner, at the age of 46, I'd really had enough of being in the marketplace as a single woman. Having woven myself a gaudy tapestry out of the romantic mismatches, disappointments and fiascos, I was eager for something more edifying. I really believed that my partner was it. Intelligent, presentable, a good listener, sexy, apparently successful. He seemed equally taken with me. Clearly, this could work. I would *make* it work.

We met through a mutual friend who fixed us up on a blind date – an expression which in the event turned out to be highly apposite, in that for a long time I was blind (wilfully so, I admit) to the signs that this relationship would lead me into new and uncharted forms of grief.

Just as my fling with a rough-cut disc jockey had been welcome for its contrast to my previous life with my husband the 'suit', so this relationship promised a refreshing change, but in a more profound way. My friend described him to me as a New Man: 'you know, the type who can cook a three-course meal *and* does the washing-up'. This sounded idyllic. My husband (one might call him Trad Man) had stopped doing anything in the kitchen the moment we got married, just as he never changed a nappy or got up in the middle of the night to feed a crying baby…but I realised he was merely following his own father's example.

Of course this New Man thing held an even greater promise than domestic chore-sharing. Namely, that we would enjoy a genuine partnership of equals – and not just because, having been born a mere two days apart, there was no possibility of an older man's paternalism. He really believed in gender equality as the ethos of the post-modern world.

Now that's all well and good. But obviously, being equal doesn't mean you are the same. And while you needn't be the same in all respects – how monotonous that would be! – it helps if you are in accord in the more crucial matters. For example, in your general outlook on the world, that all-important *Weltanschauung* which enables you truly to understand each other and connect. In this respect we were opposites. And while opposites can attract, they can just as easily repel. If your take on life, your core philosophy, constantly chafes against theirs, ultimately you are going to wear away those positive elements which attracted you to each other in the first place.

I remained committed to the relationship even as, with the passing years, it slid slowly down the pan. Because what was the alternative to keeping it together as a couple? Joining the brigade of lovelorn, single, middle-aged women who dine out and holiday together, who put a brave face on it while desperately hoping for that white knight to come galloping along at the eleventh hour? The prospect made me cringe. I found myself in the peculiar position of dreading the inevitable dissolution of this partnership, yet at the same time the thought of it lasting forever made my heart sink. In the end the decision was taken out of my hands. He simply left, it was over, and once again I was stunned by how distressing the death of even a doomed relationship can be.

By now I had begun to feel that you really could read men like a book: generally some combination of Alice in Wonderland and Dracula.

It seems that roughly every decade and a half I reinvent myself. And thus to my incarnation, at sixty, as a signed-up member of the internet dating scene, with the difference that by this stage of my life I was too battle-scarred, too cynical to believe in knights on white chargers, those mythical bearers of true love.

No, I would not be setting myself up for major disappointment. But fun and games? Uncomplicated enjoyment? Sex in the city of London? Bring it on. I would pack in as much of it as I could, while I still had the face for it, the body for it and the desire for it. After that first taste of honey, with my 26-year-old classic-film buff, I could hardly wait to see who would emerge from the ether.

CHAPTER TWO

They say that time spent in research is never wasted, but, eager to get going, I spent scant time researching the relative merits of the thousands of dating sites now proliferating on the web. After a cursory search, I alighted on one which seemed straightforward, nothing specialist (e.g. sites for chess-playing vegetarians or left-handed wine connoisseurs) and not one for 'mature' or 'senior' daters. A three-month subscription was inexpensive, and this seemed a reasonable consideration in making my choice. It wasn't one of the major, well-known sites.

I put up my profile. Everyone was anonymous, of course, going by a user-name. My user-name was Monica followed by a single-digit number chosen by the site (I wasn't its first Monica, clearly). I uploaded a modest, smiling head-and-shoulders shot. In describing myself I was honest and to the point. I said I was looking for 'some easy-going fun with the right guy'. And I gave my accurate age. Then I sat back to wait for the messages and 'winks' (the standard signal from a member who has spotted you and wants to register an interest) to ping onto my laptop.

But the responses were slow in pinging. Over the following weeks I received a trickle of interest from men in their late fifties and sixties, divorcees plus a few widowers. But their photos were unappealing and the self-describing narratives on their profiles were either dull or cheesy or just left me cold. My own searches through the database threw up similarly uninspiring cases.

Then I noticed one contender who seemed more promising. Joe49 was no youngster, his profile stated that he was 63. But he had a pleasant, intelligent-looking face, a nice head of hair (always a winner) and – a real bonus – his occupation was given as writer/journalist, same as me. He lived on the southern fringe of London, while I lived in a northern suburb, but that shouldn't pose a problem. I sent him a wink, and when after a couple of days that elicited no response, I messaged him: 'Hi there Joe. At the risk of being a bit forward, do you fancy a drink sometime? We're both journos, at the very least we can gripe about the state of the newspaper industry!'

But to my disappointment he never replied. How rude, I thought. After all, I'd only suggested a drink. I didn't say I wanted to move in and have his grandchildren. I pondered this and decided that he must have balked at my age. His profile stated that he was looking for a woman aged between 45 and 58. I wasn't too far out. But maybe he quietly preferred someone at the younger end of the scale. Nothing surprising about that.

Then I contacted another man who caught my eye, DaveTH3. He was 60, quite attractive, a company director. Not wanting to sound in any way suggestive, I simply wrote: 'Hello, I like your profile. Would you care to get together sometime for a chat over a glass of wine?' What could be more innocent? But he never sent so much as a 'no thanks'.

Meanwhile I began to receive messages from ProntoXS, 64, working in 'financial services' in Essex. Not one to hang about, from the off he announced that he would like to buy me dinner. A discerning man, clearly! But his oily-looking hair, smarmy grin and spivvy outfit gave me the creeps, so at first I ignored him. I felt a bit bad about it. Was I being unkind? He was probably a decent enough bloke. At last I sent him a polite 'thank you but I think not'. I regretted it, though, as it only encouraged him to up his game with more emphatic messages ('Try me! I'm a lot of laughs!') which was when I resorted to the ultimate sanction and blocked him from making further contact.

This was not going well.

In common with other dating sites, mine organised regular events – generally a party in some trendy bar, or a speed dating evening – at which its members could get together in the 'real world'. They could actually see and speak to each other, maybe shake hands, like people did in the old days. An appealing thought after my frustrations online. So I decided to book a place at one of their forthcoming events.

But I soon discovered that I was completely disenfranchised from them, despite being a member. They were organised along age-group lines, but the older groups into which I would naturally fit had an upper age limit for women of about 55 or 57, while men in their sixties were eligible to attend. So I was barred from making a booking. Never mind that I'm a fun gal to have around, might well have been the life and soul of the party and am reliably informed that I could pass for a much younger woman. Not one of their events was open to a woman of my age, despite the fact that my subscription fee cost just as much as that of my juniors. When I emailed the site administrators to complain, I didn't even get a reply.

I had been on the site for three weeks, hadn't been on a single date, hadn't even cyber-met anyone remotely promising and was barred from their 'fabulous' events. At this rate I was going nowhere.

It seemed to me that it was fine to be a woman in her fifties but that the dreaded number sixty put you beyond the pale. Sixty and above? Game over, lady! It was so unfair. I knew I was no different to the person I had been in my fifties. In fact I was in better shape now than earlier, whilst living with my partner, as I was consuming less and exercising more. And – despite my dislike of clothes shopping – I had invested in a fetching new wardrobe. As a journalist I was used to taking on projects, but in my new incarnation as a born-again single woman of mature years, *I* became my most important project. I would make myself as desirable as possible. I had a few good years left in me and this was my last throw of the dice in the high-stakes game of love and lust. I had forged a new 'improved formula' version of me and would not yet be put out to grass.

So I thought, right, I've had enough of this. I'll just shave a few years off my age. Big deal. Women *d'un certain âge* do that all the time. But when I tried to edit my profile details, I found I could change everything except my date of birth. I had crossed the Rubicon and there was no going back. At that point I dumped the site altogether and signed up on another.

This second site was much bigger and better known. I wrote a similar profile narrative but added the line: 'After a lot of disappointments in love, I now realise that all men are rascals [a challenging statement, if ever there was one] so I'm just looking to have a nice time with people I like' and made myself five years younger. As for my user-name, each one I came up with was already taken by someone. In the end, having grown up in New York, I called myself New Yorker (followed by the customary string of letters).

The winks were not long in arriving. The first was from a 46-year-old man who described himself as a 'cheerful cockney guy', then explained that he was born and bred in north London. I messaged him, thanking him for the wink, and joked that he couldn't be a real Cockney as he wasn't 'born within the sound of Bow bells'. At that he gruffly suggested I didn't know what I was talking about and should 'stick to New York'. So, neither Cockney nor cheerful, then. I tried replying to the touchy fellow but as he had already blacklisted me, my message didn't get through.

Good start.

After this I got a lot of attention from NorseMan, a 40-year-old Norwegian whose profile pictures showed a brawny, shaven-headed giant worthy of his pillaging ancestors. His messages to me were suggestive but just short of lewd and I was intrigued by the prospect of meeting someone so outside my normal social experience, never mind my amorous exploits. We arranged to meet for an after-work drink a few days later at a bustling bar near Oxford Circus.

I wondered what to wear and decided I needed a new summer dress, something elegant and feminine and becoming.

I found just the thing at John Lewis, and to go with it I bought a pair of wedge sandals which made me two inches taller, rather a necessity when dating a Viking.

As our assignation approached I messaged him to confirm but didn't get a reply. We hadn't exchanged mobile numbers so my only means of contacting him was through the dating site. I had misgivings, but – what did I know of Norse dating protocol? – I got ready nevertheless and took the tube into town.

I arrived at the noisy bar, on the dot, in my new outfit, perfumed and freshly coiffed. I looked around for a looming bald presence. But the Norwegian wasn't there and he didn't show up, as in my heart of hearts I had known he wouldn't.

Stood up on my very first internet date. Surely this was 'virtual' dating in its most elemental form.

I hung about for a while near the doorway, like the wallflower at the dance. Then I recalled my adolescence in suburban New York and a date I had arranged, aged 16, with a boy from another town. I had a big crush on him. He was good-looking and rich and went to a posh private school along the Hudson. A different world to mine. We were going to meet at a particular street corner where he would pick me up in his car. He didn't turn up. I was gutted and never saw him again.

But I wasn't gutted this time. From the pavement outside the bar I called a close friend who lived a few minutes' walk away, in Soho. Happily he was free that evening and we went out for a pizza, joking about the 'Scandinavian slaphead' as we got stuck into a bottle of red.

In some ways being sixty is so much better than being 16.

So far this digital dating business was a disaster. But that was to change in the blink of an eye...or more precisely, a splash in a pool.

I go to aqua-aerobics classes at my local health club several times a week. I hate using a gym but love swimming and simply being in the water, and it's a surprisingly good workout if you put some wellie in it and don't just ponce about like some of the more limp-wristed ladies in the class. If I still have a youthful figure, with flat stomach and toned limbs and sans unsightly love handles, it's largely thanks to my assiduous aqua regime. Add to that a great hairdresser and hey presto, you're away.

I had been attending the classes for a good year or so before getting cautiously friendly with some of the other women (there is a small sprinkling of men, but aqua-aerobics is primarily a female endeavour). There was one woman in particular it was impossible to miss, who stood out in every way and appeared to be on close terms with everyone. Abundantly full-bodied, with a mass of white-blonde hair and impressively sumptuous breasts, the only one to wear lipstick for aqua, Vanessa would jump gleefully into the water with an almighty splash at the start of class and her throaty laughter could be heard right across the pool. I guessed she was in her mid-fifties.

I would catch snippets of her conversations with her pals as we all leapt and lunged and twisted and twirled in the water, and they often revolved around her doings with the opposite sex. Great bosoms bouncing, her long hair in a care-less wet tangle, Vanessa was full of racy tales. The epitome of the fun-loving, single older woman gallivanting about town and firing on all cylinders.

One morning after class I joined her as she relaxed in the jacuzzi and told her about my dating disappointments. 'You're just on the wrong site, darling,' she said. (Vanessa called everyone darling.) She advised me to join the one that she had been using, on and off, for the past two years. It was more sophisticated, more London-based, and had men of a higher calibre. 'That is the place for you,' she said as she lay back smiling, blanketed in bubbles.

That afternoon I signed up on Vanessa's site for an initial three months. For good measure I took a further year off my age, making me 54. For my main profile photo I chose a black-and-white one which showed my eyes at their dark smouldering best and in which I wore an enigmatic smile. I thought carefully about my choice of user-name. What's in a name? A lot. It not only had to be to catchy, but somehow complement both the photos and the story in my narrative. I mused on this for some time before I hit on it.

The previous week I had written an article about my favourite poet, Edgar Allan Poe, for a literary magazine. Much of the piece had centred on his most famous poem, The Raven. It had meant a great deal to me in my youth, when, as a member of my high school drama group, I memorised the whole of that long, mystical and melodic poem and performed it at our end-of-year stage production. It won me the school's annual drama award. In a way, perhaps, it defined me. And so it was that I adopted the user-name Raven (which you must admit is rather sexy), explaining in my narrative its personally significant literary connotation.

Some people compose heartfelt, needy narratives on their profiles, explaining that they yearn to find their soul-mate, their 'true one', the person with whom they can share the rest of their lives, spending those special moments together curled up in front of the hearth with their cups of cocoa, chuckling at their favourite seventies sitcoms on the telly.

But that 'perfect harmony' stuff is strictly for cheesy Coca-Cola commercials. Not for me this fantasy of happy-ever-after. I reused most of New Yorker's short, snappy narrative. Nothing soppy, nothing heavy. I added the tantalising line: 'I used to be a biker chick' and uploaded a couple of supplementary photos showing me in my biking leathers. (Hey, I'm not stupid.)

Then I sat back to see how Raven got on.

CHAPTER THREE

A day or two after he stood me up NorseMan sent a feeble apology: 'Sorry I couldn't make it.' But with assholes, the best policy is to ignore them, so I didn't bother telling him off. In fact I forgot about the whole fiasco almost immediately, as New Yorker was quickly superseded by Raven. Vanessa had been right. As soon as I settled into the new site, in my new persona, the dating floodgates opened. All at once I was the most popular girl at school.

Although my first date (Viking didn't count, obviously) was never going to set my world alight. Looking at NiceMan's profile, I couldn't help but sympathise with the fellow. His unassuming narrative had gently humorous, self-deprecating touches typical of the old-school English gent. His photo depicted a slightly alarmed-looking, balding middle-aged man who, in the looks department, had much to be modest about, and he described himself as short and well-rounded, a civil servant by profession. But he seemed intelligent and amusing, so I responded to the tentative message he sent me, which began: 'Dear Raven, there are a lot of damaged souls and broken hearts out there and some of my own experiences are worthy of Edgar Allan Poe. Fall of the House of Usher comes to mind…'

We messaged a little, to and fro, employing a few literary

allusions. I told him he sounded sweet. 'Sweet?' he replied. 'Oh yeah, you say that now…' And we arranged to meet at a café in town that Friday afternoon. 'How will I know you?' I asked. 'Will you be reading a copy of Anna Karenina?' He said no, he'd probably be the one sitting there looking unhappy and 'complaining about the service'. I took that as a joke.

When I walked into the designated café and spotted a man sitting alone, our eyes met and I felt a jolt of pleasant surprise. He was no movie star but certainly nicer looking than in the profile picture. But he looked at me blankly and turned away.

Then I saw NiceMan, at a table on the opposite side of the room. He was remonstrating with the waiter about the piped music. When he saw me he stood up, but he didn't look happy. He explained that he had already moved tables once but the music was still too intrusive. Would I mind if we left that place and found somewhere else?

So we wandered off down the street. A block or two along we saw an Italian chain eatery and went inside. We sat down by the window and as soon as the waitress appeared at our table he asked her to remove the little vase containing a single dainty flower. Apparently, he didn't approve of it. I began to have doubts about the supposed niceness of NiceMan.

He didn't drink coffee or tea, so he ordered orange juice while I asked for a latte. I inquired about his job and he told me how much he hated it. He was only 50 but desperate to retire. 'It's soul-destroying in my office. Nothing works as it should. It's all public sector bullshit. I'd quit tomorrow except that I'd lose too much of my pension.' What would he do instead, if he quit his job? 'Leave London and grow vegetables.' He had never married, never had kids, never had a proper long-term relationship. So there was only himself to consider.

He had been on the dating site for six months and that, too, had been soul-destroying. 'I've lost my faith in human nature. Everyone lets you down.' He'd had a handful of dates but they didn't lead anywhere. He thought one problem was his height. He was 5 foot 6. 'It seems that no one under six feet need apply. But it normally doesn't get as far as that. Usually when somebody sees my photo I never hear from them again.' He'd had enough and had decided that when his subscription ran out he wouldn't renew. 'I'm done.' He sipped his juice gloomily, but if ever there was a person in need of a stiffer drink, it was him.

Then he recounted some cautionary tales. It seemed that a number of women on the site were Eastern Europeans hoping to acquire a UK passport through some hapless mug. And then there was a friend of his who took a glamorous young Russian woman out to dinner at the expensive restaurant she chose and plied her with champagne before discovering she was a prostitute. 'If her name is Olga you have to be very careful.' But mostly the women he had met were just callous and rude. It had been an altogether depressing experience.

I felt sorry for NiceMan. His life was a mess. And he had no one to share the mess with. But despite his generally morose air, I found myself liking him. I'm a journalist. Cynicism and world-weariness are part of my terrain. I'm at home with them. So I offered NiceMan a deal. 'Listen, to be honest with you, I don't think we're going to *go out* with each other. But we can be friends. I like talking to you. You're amusing.' (Although I wasn't sure he was all *that* amusing, in the ha-ha sense.) He smiled and paid me a compliment in return. 'Raven, I like the cut of your jib too.'

We wandered up the road towards Bond Street tube station at the end of our 'date', and agreed to meet up again as friends. He said he would like to invite me over for a home-cooked dinner. 'Lovely!' I said. And as I pushed open the glass door to the station I reasoned that it was always a good thing to enlarge my social circle. Even though that wasn't really what I'd signed up for.

SupcrA was a self-described 'North London Jew boy' used to life in the fast lane. In his late forties, he ran his own successful business in the media world, wore immaculate designer clothes and drove a classy sports car. Tall and moderately good-looking, with a neat, close-cropped beard, he was also manifestly self-satisfied. Smarmy, even. But he told funny Jewish jokes and did a brilliant Jackie Mason accent, and you can forgive a man many things if he makes you laugh.

Our first messaging session was full of good old-fashioned 'gay repartee', as though we were a latter-day Spencer Tracey and Kate Hepburn in a sophisticated forties romcom. The witty socio-cultural references! The subtle innuendos! And how refreshing to receive messages composed with perfect spelling and punctuation and grammar. You had to love these well-educated, well-read North London Jew boys.

Like NiceMan, SuperA hàd never married ('I run too fast,' he explained) or had children. But that was fine because – in common with many childless people – he claimed it was enough to have agreeable nieces and nephews. He'd been internet dating for a few years, which had led to 'some enjoyable encounters and fab sex'. I suggested that years of casual serial dating might be soul-destroying. 'Not soul-destroying,' he corrected. 'Just soulless.'

That night we graduated from messaging to texting. He set me a 'saucy quiz'. Did I prefer thongs or Bridget Jones pants? Shaved or au naturel? Missionary position or swinging from chandeliers? And so on. We had fun.

It was well past midnight by the time we packed it in. Then we fixed up a date for one night the following week. The plan was for him to come to my place following the media event he was attending in town.

I was well aware of the golden rule of internet dating: your initial meeting takes place on neutral ground, in public, with plenty of people around. Then you are safe and can make a quick getaway if necessary. You never invite someone you don't know to your own home! You don't tell him where you live! That is reckless and dangerous. Your date could be anybody. Jack the Ripper or Ted Bundy or Vlad the Impaler.

This is all wise advice.

So I gave SuperA my post code to put into his satnav and he said he would get there by 10.30.

When my partner and I split up a year earlier he moved out of the big family house we owned jointly, into rented accommodation in another part of town, and our house went on the market. But it hadn't yet sold. So I was still living there, alone amidst its spacious, partly empty rooms, once full of the sounds of family life, now quiet and secluded in a private cul-de-sac.

SuperA rolled up in his swish two-seater and parked in my drive. Laid back and courteous, he gave me a chaste kiss on the cheek before following me into the kitchen. 'Very nice,' he remarked, looking around blandly as I made us mugs of tea. Then we moved into the sitting room. He told me about his background and work, but wasn't overly curious about me, asking only a few perfunctory questions.

We started kissing, but he wasn't pushy about it and didn't do any undue groping. It went well. So after a while we moved upstairs. I can't say that Bonfire Night burst forth in my bedroom, but the experience was satisfying and comforting and pretty much what I desired just then. I felt we were companionable. As they say, we had 'clicked'. We chatted some more afterwards, he did another Jackie Mason impression which made me giggle and then we fell asleep.

In the morning he had to leave very early to get back to his house in Berkshire. Something about having a dish-washer delivered. Or perhaps it was a telly. He kissed me goodbye on the doorstep and drove off. It was 7 a.m. But I felt content as I shuffled off to the kitchen for coffee. We had already arranged to meet again the following week, in town. This time we would go out for dinner, nice bottle of wine, chat about life and get to know more about each other – the whole proper 'date' thing. A back-to-front way of going about it, maybe. But no matter. Things were defi-nitely looking up.

But my meeting with SuperA seemed far off. There was a whole weekend to get through before then and I didn't see why I should spend it alone. So, come the Saturday morning, Raven was sitting in front of the laptop having a trawl though the dating site to see who was out there. A box on one side of the page displayed small selections of men meeting my personal dating criteria, e.g. age, location, whether they were interested in a serious relationship or just a bit of fun. These were the potential dates chosen for me by the all-knowing, all-seeing site.

I saw a young face amongst these nominees. Dark blond hair and blue eyes, shy yet cheeky grin, your friendly boy-next-door. I looked at his profile. He was 23, just a baby, and his user-name, Tooting333, told me he probably lived in that South London area. Then I thought back to my life-changing, crazy (but good crazy) adventure with the 26-year-old, which had started me on this journey, and contemplated sending Tooting boy a wink. Shameless. But then, what would be the point? No doubt he would flee when he noticed my age.

I'd forgotten that people on the site can tell when someone inspects their profile.

Three minutes later a message pinged into my inbox. It was from Tooting333. 'Hi Miss Raven. How are you today? Do you have any nice plans for this weekend? I hope you don't mind me messaging but noticed you had been looking at my profile so thought I would say hello.'

Surprised and pleased, I wrote back saying I thought he was cute and that I was all in favour of younger men.

'Ah thank you. You look very pretty yourself. And I love women who are older than me. Can I ask your name? Raven sounds really cool, but is merely the name of a poem. If not I'll have to call you Miss for the time being.'

I told him my name and he told me his.

'Are you busy this weekend?,' he asked. 'Maybe we could get to know each other a bit better…' Tooting333 didn't believe in wasting time.

'What are you suggesting? Does your mum know about this?' I joked.

'I don't tell her everything!'

We agreed to meet at noon at a pub (I'll call it The Bells) in my north London neighbourhood. As I had surmised, he did live in the South London district of Tooting but was happy to travel up to me on the tube.

'Looking forward to seeing you later,' he messaged.

'All right, my frisky little pup.'

'Frisky little pup? I like that.'

He was waiting for me in the near empty pub, in his tight jeans and tee-shirt and trainers, holding a glass of beer and looking a little apprehensive. He offered to buy me a drink but that didn't seem right. (My instinct when with young people, unless they were Justin Bieber or something, was to pay for things.) So I went to the bar and got my own glass of wine, then sat down opposite him.

Slowly we broke the ice of what we both recognised as a highly irregular situation. As he warmed to our conversation about his work (in accountancy) and his family (from Lancaster), and I told him something of my own life, and we sipped our drinks and shared bar snacks, his shyness began to fade and he smiled more.

I liked his informal yet respectful manner. He was bright, thoughtful and knowledgeable (his copy of The Times, his Saturday reading matter of choice, lay on the seat beside him).

He had only ever had one girlfriend, briefly, at university, and by and large he wasn't interested in girls of his own age. 'All they want to talk about is the X Factor and the latest celebrity gossip or silly stuff about past boyfriends.' The other problem was that they wanted to get too serious too soon: 'After a couple of dates they start putting on the pressure. They want a proper relationship and commitment. I say "Slow down, you hardly know me," and they say "Yeah but you're so nice..."' He shrugged.

'So at that point you give them the chop?'

He smiled. 'Yeah.'

I could see the attraction for him of the older woman. He didn't have to spell it out.

The afternoon flowed easily by and at 3.30 we strolled back to my place for tea. I wondered what the next step in this unfamiliar scenario might be. What was he expecting? Wanting? I had no idea. He was far too well-behaved to 'make a move' on me. At that moment I wasn't feeling at all worldly. Help!

'What would you like to do now?' I asked, not meeting his eyes, feeling embarrassed and hoping it didn't show too much.

'Give me your hands,' he said, and he took them gently and held them, reassuring me. 'We'll do whatever *you* want

34

to do.' I was nearly forty years his senior. How come he was being more grown up about this than me? I gave his fingers a squeeze, followed by a sly grin.

I think I had been expecting Tooting333's performance in bed to be puppy-like – raw and awkward, all enthusiasm and little know-how. But I couldn't have been more wrong. Although he was young and had had very few sexual partners, he displayed a deeper understanding of the act than many men – most men, perhaps – twice his age. Tender and sensual and generous, he was simply a natural. The incredible, many would say absurd, age gap between us didn't enter into the equation. I don't think either of us thought about it for a second.

I found his healthy, strong body very appealing. I complimented him on his super-muscular thighs and he told me they were a result of his football playing; he belonged to a team in south London and played on weekends. (As a teenager I had a friend called Esther who, as a pretty seventeen-year-old, went on holiday with her parents to the Algarve. She met George Best on the beach one night and they had sex. 'His thighs were like rocks,' she said admiringly. I finally knew what she meant.)

Later that evening we went downstairs and ate a dinner of spaghetti and ice cream in the sitting room while watching a silly film on the telly. And we laughed and sprawled on the sofa like a pair of teenagers.

He stayed over that night and fell asleep with his head nestling on my shoulder. And the next morning he left for Tooting.

He sent me a text from the tube station. 'Hi Miss. It's L'il Pup here. Lovely seeing you. Hope to see you again soon.'

From then on I always called him Pup and he generally referred to me as Miss. I loved the vaguely Benny Hill sauciness of it.

'I'll do anything you want, Miss.'

Bloody hell.

CHAPTER FOUR

$\mathcal{V}$anessa's dating site was proving to be highly fertile ground. Even before my upcoming second get-together with SuperA on Friday, I had organised a dating double-whammy for one midweek evening.

My first assignation was for cocktails at the popular bar-café over-looking Piccadilly from the top floor of the Waterstones flagship store. My date was with Ramon, a 48-year-old South American businessman. Darkly handsome, in his outdoorsy photos he resembled a rugged, bearded mountaineer. This macho appearance was at odds with the affected language he used in his on-site messages. Referring to the line in my narrative about all men being rascals, he countered with: 'Laying the cards down, I struggle to refrain myself from coming to the quite generalised negative view about the opposite sex as well. I'm on the cusp of concluding that all women are heartless. It could be fun to share our case folders.'

I told him that only a heartless woman could refuse his proposal. '*Touché!*' he responded. 'I have another meeting that day which flutters like a butterfly and I don't know what time it will land. Yet a glass at the end of a warm day as the night cold begins to nibble is a glorious time.'

Jesus, I thought. He could be hard work.

We agreed to meet at six o'clock. He told me to look for someone 'most likely staring at an iPhone, thoroughly detached from his surroundings (some might say, disembodied)'. A description which nowadays would hardly narrow the field.

As I stepped out of the lift I spotted him soon enough, staring into his iPhone. As I approached he glanced up and gave me a smile. Still uncertain of the protocol on these occasions I reached out to shake his hand, but he took me by the shoulders and kissed me on both cheeks.

We ordered mojitos and started chatting. Like many passionate entrepreneurs Ramon could wax lyrical about the challenges of start-ups and 'high-risk strategies', and expound at length on 'growing an SME', 'taking the business to new levels' and the intricacies of recapitalisation. I tried not to let my eyes glaze over. My ex was a business consultant and I'd been listening to the yawn-inducing jargon for many years. But at least the ex hadn't larded his talk with Ramon's flowery, faux-poetic expressions.

At last he showed a modicum of polite interest in me and my own career. He was, after all, a man of breeding, the son of a former government minister and privately educated. And so we carried on conversing for the next hour or so (with me trying to keep it all in plain English) before he had to head off to watch some art-house film with a friend. We exchanged more cheek-kisses as we said good-bye and said we would meet up again. But I suspected we wouldn't. It had been a friendly encounter but as they say in this game, 'there was no spark'. Our personalities were not a good fit. And despite his rugged Latin looks I found Ramon strangely sexless.

The mojitos had been good, though, and I was reasonably well-oiled for my second date of the evening. This was with Jock (roughly the same age as Ramon), a burly, six foot three inch Scot and yet another beardy. I had never particularly liked facial hair and it was becoming strangely difficult to escape. Jock worked for a private equity company and lived in the Docklands. He had laid on the charm in his messages to me, complimenting me on my looks and 'fantastic smile' (which he followed with that tedious smiley-face symbol, as if to hammer home the point).

Jock lived in a high-rise block with a swimming pool and suggested I bring my bikini so he could check out the tan I mentioned I'd recently acquired in my garden. But I had had an expensive blow-dry that day and wasn't about to spoil my hair in a pool. So we were meeting for drinks and a bite at one of the many Docklands hang-outs teeming with bonus-fed suits in 'financial services'.

It had started to rain lightly and I reckoned I might as well have gone for that swim. Jock met me at the tube station (a process which took some time as, ridiculously, he was waiting somewhere out of sight) and ushered me through revolving doors into a packed bar. As we settled in a corner with our drinks, he turned his solemn gaze on me. He was less charming and more taciturn in person than he had been online. Neither bad-looking nor good-looking. One of those.

We discussed our respective circumstances and he explained that his divorce had recently come through from his wife, who he described as greedy and calculating. She had really made him pay. The proceedings had dragged on for ages and their rapacious lawyers had made things worse.

I made a few ironic asides about divorce and relationships, but they fell flat, as he clearly didn't 'get them'. In fact Jock didn't smile much at all and his pale eyes studied me closely, almost as if I were his prey, which I found faintly exciting.

When we had finished our food and drinks he invited me up to his 'apartment' for coffee. He lived high up, he told me, with great views of the river, the O2 Centre and boats and things. I knew exactly what he was inviting me up for but at that moment I considered only that I had never been in one of those glittering Docklands towers with their swanky lobbies and panoramic views. A coffee? Sure, why not?

The outlook from his windows was indeed impressive, although I had to twist my neck around to left and right to see the promised sights. Because dead ahead was another great glass tower, an office block with a million windows staring straight into his butch, no-frills sitting room and I wondered how he ever got any privacy. I sat down on his black leather sofa, leaned back and yawned. Dating was tiring.

He made us mugs of coffee, put them down on the glass table before us and seated himself close to me with an expectant look on his face. I took a few sips. Then he asked me what I wanted to do.

'Dunno,' I said, as I drank a little more coffee and gave him a noncommittal glance. Whereupon he abruptly took hold of my face and landed a big messy kiss on my mouth. Such a cliché that I laughed. Then without further ado he lifted me up and carried me off to his bedroom, like some Neanderthal carting off a helpless female consort to his cave. He lowered me onto the bed in his equally masculine bedroom, all dark wooden built-in furniture, vast TV screen and state-of-the-art gizmos.

Jock was a robust and practised shagger, in the way that most feral animals are. Hump hump hump. And the delicate chain necklace he wore was markedly incongruous with his caveman behaviour.

Three nocturnal humping sessions later, as the early morning light crept into his 'apartment', I felt drained and achy and ready to go home. At intervals during the night his various gadgets – phone, computer, god-knows-what – made urgent little bleeps and pips, waking me with a start each time, while he slumbered on. Apparently he never switched anything off.

When Jock, clad in huge, fluffy white dressing gown, finally got out of bed and disappeared into his butch bathroom – seemingly in no hurry to come out – I slowly rose and put my clothes on.

A little later we drank tea and I peered out at the myriad windows opposite, now with office workers moving behind them. Jock spoke in a monotone about his neighbours, who were mainly foreign. They were all right, he said. Unobtrusive. He said he liked living in Docklands and I began to understand why. The area was as cold and impersonal as him.

He gave me an empty peck on the cheek as I left and closed the door behind me. As I wandered down long beige hallways looking for the lift, I remembered my time with Little Pup. What a blinding contrast to the Jock experience. Really, I would have to be more discriminating. And no more of this sex on the first date nonsense. (Unless I really fancied it, obviously.) In any case, I knew I wouldn't be coming back to this place. Observing Jock in the harsh morning light, as he lay in bed, snoring, legs akimbo, I realised I didn't fancy it with him at all.

I'm sitting in the kitchen with my tall, blonde daughter-in-law Sara, 34. She's also my confidante. I certainly tell her more about my doings than I tell any of my friends. She is not only astute but ultra-discreet and I trust her implicitly. We have periodic pow-wows over a bottle of wine at which we discuss how my internet dating is coming along, and one recurrent theme is how much I should tell my two sons, the older of which is her husband. She thinks I should keep it on a strictly need-to-know basis, and that they needn't know very much. I agree. For a start, I think it might freak out my sons to know about my coupling with Little Pup, who is considerably younger than they are. Sara, on the other hand, is full of admiration for this development. I think she rather enjoys having a mother-in-law who cooks a traditional Sunday roast for the family one week and gets it on with a cute 23-year-old the next.

But now she eyes me with consternation and shakes her head. 'How could you just go to his place like that, on the first date? He could have been a psycho. Could have done anything he wanted to you.' She is referring to Jock. I try to explain that I acted on gut instinct, made a judgement call, and that at my advanced age I felt I was good at evaluating people, which gave me confidence and a sense of security. 'I mean, yes it was rather a mindless hump-fest, but Jock wasn't *dangerous*.' But I know Sara is right. I had been silly and rash. I am not an infallible judge of character; no one is.

Neither does she think it was clever of me, the other night, to invite SuperA over to my house, sight unseen. Another potential axe-murderer. I squirm under her disapproving gaze.

'From now on,' Sara says, 'just as a precaution, text me whenever you go on a date, with details of the meeting-place, the time, the fellow's name. Then send an "all-safe" text afterwards to let me know you got home okay. Otherwise I'll have to inform the police and you might get your door kicked in the next day.'

I laugh. I know this is the protocol amongst some internet daters. Women looking out for each other. And I appreciate Sara's care and concern. But she is the mother of two small children and drops into bed exhausted by 9.30 most evenings, so I doubt she would be aware of whether or not I'd sent her a late night 'all-safe'. I give her a hug and promise to be more prudent. And the irony of our role reversal isn't lost on either of us.

The day before my awaited dinner date with SuperA, he texted to let me know he wouldn't be able to make it. He had unexpectedly been swamped with work and for the next fortnight would have no time for anything else. He was really sorry, as he had been looking forward to it, but he'd be in touch to rearrange as soon as the pressure was off. He ended with the customary XXs.

I felt a pang of disappointment. I believed there was a real connection between us and was eager to build on it. But I understood about work constraints and wanted him to see just how understanding I was. 'I'm sorry too, but no problem.

Hope the new assignment goes well and looking forward to seeing you at the end of it. XX.'

Naturally I was surprised and dismayed when, logging on to the dating site the following morning, I noticed him online. (It's always flagged up when a member is logged on, so that it is clear who is currently available for potential 'real time' flirtation.) I also felt another emotion I hadn't experienced for a while: jealousy. And I hated it.

I hammered out a curt, resentful message. 'Busy working, are we? You men are all the same.'

Back came his immediate rejoinder. 'Beg your pardon? What's that supposed to mean?'

'Do whatever you like, it's all the same to me. But I've had enough of men bullshitting me.'

'What's this outburst about?'

'It's fine if you want to trawl around the site looking for females to cavort with but a little honesty would be nice. Needn't pretend to be out of action due to work. Just say you've got other fish to fry. As for me, I'm out. Not interested any more.'

'I'm not trawling, just politely answering a few messages. What has this got to do with whether I'm working or not and why are you so pissed off? I haven't been dishonest with you. I'm mystified as to what I've done wrong!'

'You gave the impression you were too busy to draw breath for a fortnight. So I was surprised to find you on the dating scene.'

'Well, unusually for a man, I can multi-task. And I don't appreciate being berated by you.'

End of conversation. And with that it appeared my

'relationship' with SuperA was over before it had really begun.

Why was I upset? I had hardly known him. Obviously I had read too much into the easy connection we'd made between us. I had thought it promising, but in reality there had been no promise. And I concluded that the reason for his lack of interest in the details of my life was that, the less he knew, the looser the connection, the easier it would be for him to cut me off when he decided my time was up. Maybe that was simply the way internet dating worked for him, and probably for most other men too.

As for me, the answer was not to care so much. After all, there was an abundant supply of willing men out there in cyberspace, as I was beginning to see. No point in crying over any one of them. From now on I would endeavour to stick to that principle. I'd toughen up. No more getting upset or jealous, no more being outwardly insouciant while remaining an unreconstructed old softie inside.

CHAPTER FIVE

*A*t this point my escapades took an ethnic turn. I'd been receiving copious attention from a 56-year-old Indian architect called Jabir, who was divorced with three grown children. He bombarded me with messages that were way over-the-top effusive, jasmine-scented and sickly sweet: 'Hello beautiful young lady, sweetheart and delicious one.' And the next day: 'Hello again, you clever little angel with beautiful eyes. How are you on this fine sunny day?' And the next: 'What are you doing on this gorgeous day, my gorgeous dear friend? Had lunch yet? Anything yummy? XXXX.' And all this before we had even met.

His profile narrative said all the right things about how trustworthy and responsible he was, warm-hearted and considerate, etc. The usual spiel. And his picture showed a presentable, well-dressed man with swept-back dark hair, smiling broadly for the camera. So despite his tiresome Bollywood-style effusions, and in the interests of multiculturalism, I agreed to have dinner with him, choosing my favourite Indian restaurant in north London. He seemed pleasant enough, and it would be a new experience for me. I'd never had a date with an Indian fella.

We had arranged to meet at the restaurant at 7.30 p.m. But at 6 p.m. on the evening in question Jabir texted me to ask whether our date was for 6.30 or 7.30. I answered that it was 7.30. 'Well,' he replied, 'I am there already.' There already? What would he do at the restaurant on his own for an hour and a half? He didn't seem very organised. I told him I couldn't get there before 7.30. 'Okay, see you in a while you gorgeous crocodile!' he texted.

But when I turned up, on the dot, I was perturbed to see that he wasn't there at all. I sat down to wait. After five minutes I dashed off an irate text. A further five minutes later he arrived at last in a fluster. It turned out that he had been waiting across the road in McDonald's, drinking tea and sitting by the window, ostensibly keeping an eye on the restaurant entrance for my arrival. Which he had failed to notice.

Clearly this would never do.

Wearing a shiny brown suit, Jabir took his seat opposite me and I could tell straight away he was not in jolly Bollywood mood. And if his brusque manner towards the waiting staff was anything to go by, he was not as 'warm-hearted and considerate' as he had painted himself. To be frank, he was also more ropey-looking than on his photo. His hair had thinned, he appeared haggard, and in place of the attractive smile with its even rows of white teeth, there was a dark, decaying hole on one side where a tooth should have been. I suspected this sight would put me off my food and was tempted to get up and leave. But there was enough of the old Ms Softie in me to stay, albeit with sinking heart.

On the upside, he had dropped the earlier toe-curling, gushy tone of his messages.

Being an Indian, I had assumed Jabir was Hindu. But it transpired that he was Muslim. We started discussing current affairs and various socio-political issues, and had opposing views on every single one of them. Put simply, he blamed George W. Bush for virtually all the ills of the world. And I didn't. This was never going to be a meeting of minds. But I didn't want an all-out row.

So I changed tack and asked about his dating experiences, and right away things became more interesting. He had been on the site for eight months, he said, and met a number of women, all in their fifties. Most, he said, were 'desperate for physical intimacy, sex, TLC'.

One woman, who as it happened was Jewish, came out with an overt sexual proposal on their first date: 'She asked me what is my favourite position in bed, and are there any special kinky things I like. But I didn't accept her invitation. I said "Miriam, this talk is unbecoming to a nice lady like you." Unfortunately I had given her my phone number and she called me a few times in the middle of the night. Thank god I didn't give her my address or she would have showed up at my door.'

Other women he dated, he said, were just 'very stupid. They wanted to talk about silly things, but knew nothing of world events. If I said to them, "I wonder whether Kim Jong-un will start a world war," they looked at me blankly with no clue what I am talking about.' I started warming to the guy, a little.

Then he recounted the story of the stunning 25-year-old blonde on the site who one day winked and messaged him warmly. He responded in kind, immediately smitten. (I could easily imagine it: 'Hello gorgeous, beautiful, angelic-looking young lady, delicious, yummy yummy, how are you today and what's for lunch? XXXX.') She was foreign and a little vague when asked about her background, but he guessed she was Eastern European. Once they had exchanged mobile numbers her messages became more 'sexually suggestive' and he got hot under the collar, reckoning his luck was in. They set up a rendezvous at a big shopping centre on the northern outskirts of London.

He waited a long time for her at the agreed meeting place, but she never showed up. Later she rang to apologise: she'd been called away suddenly, her mother had suddenly been taken ill. Any bozo would have seen through that hackneyed pretext. But Jabir believed her: 'I said, oh please don't worry, that's fine, mothers are very important, one's sick mother must always come first.' Whereupon the beauteous Cossack, or whatever she was, assured him that she was still keen to meet and gave him her new mobile number, urging him to call her soon.

'A few days later I rang this number and another woman answered. We talked and talked and I realised it was a kind of sexual services number and the woman asked me what kind of service I would like, full-body massage, etc., and she went through a long list and told me how much each one cost. I declined all of them of course, but it was embarrassing and I found it difficult to get off the phone. Eventually, after maybe half an hour, I hung up. And when my phone bill arrived I saw that the call cost me nearly £40.'

I frowned at him, lost for words. Jabir was au fait with world events. He knew all about the war-mongering tendencies of Kim Jong-un. But when it came to scams, there was no greater mug.

He admitted that, on reflection, it wasn't likely that a gorgeous pouting 25-year-old (or in reality, perhaps, some ugly pock-marked con artist from the Caucasus) would throw herself at a middle-aged Indian divorcee living in Pinner.

When dinner was over and he had paid the bill and given me a box of high-quality chocolates as a present (a surprising move which I found quite touching), we made our way outside and he walked me to my car. We said how nice it had been to meet, interesting chat, lovely food and all that, said good-bye and shook hands. We knew we would not meet again.

The next day I texted to thank him for the dinner and wish him happiness for the future. In the end, he had proved to be gentleman. I just hoped he did something about that missing tooth. He had no chance of finding a girlfriend before then. None at all.

My multicultural dating continued apace. The day after my dinner with Jabir I had a date with a Turk whose user-name was the über-cheesy HelloToYou. A bespectacled, 34-year-old sales manager, he had been sending me earnest, detailed messages on a regular basis, filling me in on his daily activities, his work, holiday plans, sporting endeavours and opinions on the weather. Too much information, so I ignored most of them.

One of his messages had read: 'I am looking for a serious, long-term relationship. But I realise that with our age gap it is less likely to be serious and permanent and more likely to be a casual one (at least at the start) but I don't believe that's necessarily a bad thing. As long as we are both single and the chemistry exists, we can see how it goes, share quality time with respect, honesty and dignity. I am not after a one-night stand or a fling, though. Let's meet and see if we are on the same page.'

In the end, after several entreaties (yes, ever the softie) I decided to give him a chance and agreed to meet for a drink. At The Bells. He seemed a well-disposed, if unexciting, bloke. Anyway, it was only a drink at my local.

I found a seat at an outdoor table and waited for HelloToYou, who informed me he'd be a little late as he was held up in traffic. A young black man in a leather jacket sat opposite me, talking and laughing into his mobile. He was telling a mate about a woman he'd recently met. He gave her 'nine out of ten', as I couldn't help but hear. I glanced at him from time to time. He had an attractive smile.

At last HelloToYou arrived. He was shorter and slighter than I had expected, and even more staid. He bought us drinks and sat down next to me – a little too close perhaps – and we began talking about ourselves and what we hoped to get out of online dating. The black guy, who had by now finished chatting on his mobile, glanced over at us, his interest roused.

I explained that I was taking the dating lightly, not searching for anything too intense, no serious long-term commitment, no, not me. Meanwhile he studied me intensely and seriously, while edging even closer so that our thighs were almost touching. My personal space was disappearing rapidly and I wanted it back. When I glanced up at the black guy, our eyes met and a faint smile flickered across his lips.

My date then launched into a lengthy amplification of his position. He was after a love affair with 'honesty and trust', whether long or short, it was the quality that mattered, the passion. He found the idea of intimacy between a young man and older woman 'very sexy', he said. Then he added that he thought I was the right woman for him and we should try it.

How could I tell him that I too found the idea of that kind of intimacy sexy, but that he was far from *my* ideal candidate? For me – as for most people, I believe – physical attraction is a sine qua non. And I didn't fancy him one iota. To boot, his personality was strangely colourless. So I suggested that we could be friends. A lame idea, admittedly, but I felt cornered with nowhere else to go, and anyhow, that approach seemed to work with NiceMan. But he dismissed the suggestion. 'I'm not sure we're on the same page,' he observed mournfully. Same page? Not even in the same book, mate! I wanted to say.

At this point I looked at the black guy again and he winked at me. Now there's somebody who *is* fanciable and looks like good fun, I thought. Why can't I be having a drink with him?

HelloToYou remarked that the only basis on which he would agree that we positively *weren't* on the same page (that tedious expression again) was if I told him that I felt there was no chemistry between us. That he could accept. So I took the bull by the horns and said, 'Look, I think you're a nice man and I'm sure the lady you're searching for is out there somewhere. But it's not me, because I don't believe there *is* any chemistry between us.'

He nodded slowly and said 'Okay.' I felt a welcome wave of relief, like when you take off a bra that's too tight and you can breathe freely again. A few minutes later we stood up and it was good-bye to you, HelloToYou. As I turned to leave I threw one last look at the cool black dude and we smiled at each other conspiratorially. A delicious moment and one I suspected he would soon be sharing with his mate on the mobile. Which was fine by me.

I was beginning to see that internet dating was rather like shopping for clothes in a charity store. It was a good idea, and ploughing through all the weird, odd-smelling stuff was a bit of an adventure, but you were only too aware that finding something you liked was going to be a tough call.

The following week I had a date with a Frenchman. This internet dating business was fabulously cosmopolitan, I told myself.

Édouard was in his mid-fifties, another divorcee, urbane and Continental in his manners. He had proposed that we meet to share a bottle of chilled French white at a bar in swinging Notting Hill. It was a warm sunny evening and we sat at an outdoor table in our sunglasses, chatting about our families, past relationships and work (Édouard was in advertising).

Our initial online conversation, a week or so previously, had gone well. 'I love the name Monica,' he wrote in one message. 'As I held the hand of a girl named Monica when I was eight years old!' *Oo-la-la*. When I mentioned that I was relaxing and sipping a glass of wine at my desk after a long day's work, he asked: 'What are you drinking, red or white?'

'Red, Édouard. A nice little Fleurie. And feeling better already.'

'Red is good. Although a fine white, Sancerre or Chablis, can "lift me higher", to put it in a flowery way, without being a writer. Let us reconvene soon to have a glass or two of Sancerre...or Chablis...'

Something of a connoisseur, then, with Gallic charm. And while he was no Alain Delon, the face in his photos was unlikely to frighten the horses. All in all, it boded well. And now here we were, basking in the west London sunshine.

After our wine-drinking we decided to amble off in search of a light supper. We entered a noisy eatery off Portobello Road. It was packed with young trendies and we joked about being the oldest people there.

As we ate our steamed monkfish with sautéed beet greens and sipped a chilled summery rosé, we carried on talking – about our travels and the differences between Continental and British cultures, and then, inevitably, about some of the people we had encountered through internet dating. I can't say I felt a sexual spark between us, but I enjoyed his sophisticated company and our freewheeling conversation.

It was still only 9 p.m. by the time we rose to leave. He walked out of the restaurant in front of me and as I watched him from behind, I noticed for the first time his slightly bow-legged old-man's gait, like someone with gammy knees perhaps, or a dodgy back. Now he really did seem out of place in that hipster hang-out. It might sound shallow, but I knew I could never be romantically involved with someone who walked like that. Sorry!

We said good-bye at a street corner; I was going one way

and he the other. We pecked at each other's cheeks, agreed that it had been a lovely evening and that next time we'd go to a restaurant a little more in tune with our own style and generation. I wasn't sure there *would* be a next time, if only because we didn't seem fated to become anything more than casual friends. But that was all right. I reckoned he was the sort of chap I could one day invite over to a drinks party in the garden, to add a French touch to the proceedings.

A few days later, whilst perusing the dating site, I saw Édouard's profile and decided to dispatch a friendly note. 'Hello, hope you're enjoying the summer. Been drinking any nice Chablis?' But a box popped up on my screen with an astonishing message: 'Sorry, this member has blocked you from making further contact.' I stared at it. What the fuck? I said out loud.

I wracked my brains to think what could have caused him to take this draconian step. It had been an agreeable evening. Was it something I had said? I'm pretty sure I resisted the temptation to be rude about the French. Something I had done? Or did I have beet greens stuck between my teeth?

Then it occurred to me that he might have blocked me by mistake. Inadvertently clicked on some bit of the website. So I texted him: 'Hi Édouard. Did you mean to block me on the dating site? If so, it's fine, I'm just curious as to why.'

The damned frog never even replied. So, no mistake then. Maybe there were just some weird aspects to this internet dating business that I had yet to figure out.

And I was about to learn exactly how weird it could get.

CHAPTER SIX

A wink pinged onto my laptop and when I entered the site to see who had sent it, I found MaxE8. He was English, aged 30 and six feet tall. A graphic designer living in the East End. I was enjoying this attention from young men, and MaxE8 was attractive, even-featured, his dark hair worn spiky on top, the way young men often do, to give them that slightly bad-boy look. And there was a mischievous glint in his eyes. In short, he was sexy. And after my past three encounters, all I could think was *vive la différence.*

His profile contained the standard stuff about enjoying going out with friends to restaurants and pubs and films, while also being happy to stay in with a DVD and a pizza and the 'right girl', and how he liked to keep fit and was hard-working but also adventurous and open-minded. I'd read it all before. But at the end he had added: 'There is more to me than meets the eye.' Intriguing!

I winked back at MaxE8 and soon afterwards he sent me a message to ask how I was finding the site and what I was looking for, signing it 'Max'. I said I was just after a little fun following the end of a long, difficult relationship. 'Fun sounds good,' he replied. 'Maybe we could have that together…' Wha-hey!

I told him I was fond of younger men and he answered

that, as he was fond of older women, we might be suited to each other. This was getting better and better. 'You look great for your age,' he said.

'What do you mean, for my age? Ha ha…' And so we carried on for a while and I was enjoying the flirtatiousness of our exchanges. When I mentioned that I liked swimming he said he did too but that maybe we should try the hot tub together instead.

We agreed to meet for a drink the following Saturday evening and he took my mobile number, saying he would text me later that night.

At about 11 p.m. I was lying in bed surrounded by my usual accoutrements: newspapers and magazines, books, Filofax (I can be so quaint), notebook and pen, radio remote control, mobile phone, mug of peppermint tea.

My mobile tinkled with the arrival of a text. It was Max. Gone was the more understated tone of our earlier online chat. Flirty had given way to dirty. His opening gambit was: 'Looking forward to ripping your knickers off, sexy!'

A part of me – the 60-year-old grandmother part, I suppose – thought I ought to be offended. Did he think I was some floozy? But I couldn't get uptight about it. A hot-looking guy half my age fancied me. It was exciting and heady. So I took it as a compliment. And anyway, hadn't I set myself up for this?

'Ooh, hold that thought.' I texted back.

Max had other thoughts, too. Including some very naughty ones involving threesomes. His favoured scenario involved us getting into bed with a 'slutty 18-year-old'. Clearly, we weren't 'on the same page'.

'I think you'll have to do that with some other older woman!' I tapped out.

'How about a horny 18-year-old guy then? You would enjoy the kinkiness of it.' Jesus. Compared to this, SuperA's 'saucy quiz' was like something out of Dennis the Menace.

'Maybe I'm not quite your type, Max. I'm a bit classier than that. Let's concentrate on us instead of involving third parties.'

'That's fine. But you still like kinky naughty stuff, right?'

'Up to a point. But there's got to be some affection too, otherwise it's soulless. Know what I mean?'

He didn't answer that.

'I want to kiss you passionately,' he went on. 'As an older woman you can instruct me on how to kiss you. I think we'll be attracted to each other. Don't you?'

'Yes, but I need to like you, as well.'

'Well I hope you like me then!'

'Me too. Meanwhile, don't think mindless shagging. Think making love. That's so much better.'

And after a pause: 'Do you want me to call you mummy when we're making love?'

'Oh for chrisssakes! No I do not!'

'Just an idea.'

'A dopey one. Right, I'm off to sleep. Good-night!'

I liked his fervour but he was definitely an unorthodox one, that Max, definitely 'adventurous and open-minded' as per his dating profile. Still, as the senior partner in this little liaison, the older woman who he said could 'instruct him', I reckoned I could rein in his wilder appetites.

But first we would have to meet for that drink and take

the measure of each other. So on Saturday evening I headed back to The Bells.

I was sitting on a bar stool, sipping a glass of iced Zinfandel, when he walked in. Tall and cool, wearing jeans and a tight-fitting hoody which showed off his fit young body, and sunglasses which he took off so that he could wink at me. He looked even hotter than I'd expected. He kissed my cheek, murmured 'All right?', and ordered himself a beer. Oh yes. I was going to enjoy this date.

We sat down at a table and he started talking, easily enough, about his life. He liked his job but wanted to start his own design business one day so he could be his own boss. He said he enjoyed living in the East End – such a great area for creative types like him. And he explained that he grew up in Bristol and his parents were divorced. 'Everyone's parents are divorced now, right?' he quipped. He said he never wanted to get married or even live with anyone. 'I couldn't do that,' he said, rather too definitively, I thought.

Then he abruptly stopped talking, stood up and announced: 'I'm going outside for a smoke.' And before I knew it he was gone, leaving me sitting alone, glass in hand, at the table. A bit odd. And he was away a long time. Had he changed his mind about me and gone home?

But at last he returned, sat back down and flashed me a smile, and we picked up where we had left off. A moment later he said: 'I'm starving. Should we eat something?' So we ordered sausages and mash from the bar and as we ate our meal I stole glances at him, marvelling at the turn of events which had led to my date with a young hunk like Max, when only a few months earlier I had feared my dating days were over.

By this point I knew I'd be inviting him back to my place. I was dying for a snog. When we had finished our meal and came to a natural break in our chat, I gave him what I hoped was an alluring smile. 'So…wanna come up and see my etchings?'

He looked confused. 'Etchings.' He frowned as if trying to work out whether we had mentioned etchings earlier in the conversation.

Obviously he had never heard the expression. Wrong generation. Perhaps I'd better not refer to Private Eye's 'Ugandan discussions', either.

'What I mean is, fancy some coffee at my place?'

'Yeah.' He gathered his things and stood up. We stopped at the bar to pay the bill, which was handed to me, as the tab was on my credit card. 'I'll give you the cash,' he said, already making his way towards the door and taking another cigarette out of his pocket. I paid and followed him out.

We walked back to my house, less than ten minutes away, and when we got there I led the way into the kitchen, turned on the radio for some easy-listening music and reached for the percolator. But he wasn't bothered about any of that. He took me by the arms and gave me a long and zealous kiss. Afterwards he had a look around and observed approvingly that the place was clean and tidy.

We got touchy-feely again and it wasn't long before we headed upstairs. But once there, he did something unusual. While I entered my bedroom, expecting him to follow me in, he went off instead to peer into every other first-floor room, to 'see what's in them'. Like an estate agent sizing up a property for sale...which was what my house was, of course.

'They're just bedrooms,' I called out, baffled. Maybe he was interested in the housing market? Or was he worried about possible strangers lurking in this big silent house?

Turning lights on and off in various rooms, he satisfied himself that there was nothing untoward going on. But when he saw children's cots and toys in one of the bedrooms, he turned to me curiously and asked about them.

'Grandchildren,' I said. Now I knew I had to divulge my real age. Otherwise the numbers just wouldn't add up. 'Max, I'm a little older than it says on my profile.'

'Oh? How much older?'

'Um...59.'

He eyed me shrewdly. 'You're sixty, aren't you?'

I sighed and gave up. 'Yup.' I paused. 'Is that a problem?'

I was expecting some show of disappointment, maybe even antipathy. But his mouth formed into a wicked grin and he said, 'A 60-year-old granny. Even kinkier.' And he kissed me again, hard.

Lying in bed, I watched Max take off his clothes and lay them down neatly in a row on the floor. That's when he mentioned his OCD. And suddenly it all made sense. The examining of the rooms, the preoccupation with tidiness, the blunt statement about not being able to live with anyone. When he had mentioned during our meal that he never cooked because he didn't want to get his kitchen utensils dirty, I'd laughed because I thought he was joking.

So. OCD. That must have been what he meant about

there being more to him 'than meets the eye'. Must be tricky to live with, I thought. What a palaver. I had never before observed this condition at such close quarters. But after years on Fleet Street there wasn't much about the human race that could surprise or shock me. I could handle it. If this was as bad as it got.

But then it got worse.

Max was a forceful sex partner, strong and insistent. I didn't mind that – although a little tenderness would not have gone amiss – because, like most women, I'm partial to the occasional 'bit of rough'. But he took it too far, going at it with as much obsession as he put into his orderliness with clothes and kitchen utensils.

Pinning me down on the bed, he looked into my eyes and said the one word I had hoped he wouldn't utter. *Mummy.*

'Are you enjoying this, *mummy*?' His face was only an inch from mine.

I closed my eyes. 'Don't say that.' I turned away and squirmed underneath him. 'I'm *not* your mummy.'

'But he wouldn't stop. 'You like it, don't you, mummy?'

'*No,*' I breathed up at him. I found this role-playing unnerving. Raunchy is good. A bit of manhandling is fine. But this mother-son fantasy was not at all fine. It was warped. Christ, we were *so* not on the same page.

'I'm your *boy*, aren't I? Say I'm you're boy.' He put his hand around my throat and squeezed hard. When, after a few seconds, he didn't let go I tried to prise his fingers off my neck but it wasn't easy. I was finding it hard to breathe. It was as if he really meant business and that unnerved me.

When he finally loosened his grip I said, trying to be

reasonable and calming, 'Come on Max, you don't really want to choke me, do you?'

He said nothing after that but kept his hand on my throat a while longer, pressing a little too tightly for comfort, and I pulled at his fingers. At long last he reached his climax, let go of me and fell back on the bed in a sweat.

And as I lay there recovering from these exertions, all I could think was: what the FUCK would Freud make of that? Perhaps Max had already found some creepy women prepared to play the mummy game, women who even enjoyed it, and he thought I wouldn't mind. Wrong.

Later that night there was another, less edgy session, without the role-playing this time. Then we fell asleep.

Early in the morning I tiptoed downstairs to make myself coffee. I drank it out in the garden, breathing in the cleansing fresh air. I pondered on the dicey doings of the previous night. Wow, I'd really taken a risk this time. How stupid. In future I would have to be more cautious. I dreaded to think what Sara would have to say about this episode.

Max came down a little later, dressed and ready to leave. After gulping down a coffee he said he had better go, it was a long way back to Hackney.

I dropped him off at the tube station and before he got out of my car he gave me a peck on the lips and muttered, 'I'll call you'. But he didn't sound as if he would and I hoped he wouldn't. As he strode off, wearing his shades, I reflected that although he was a sicko, he was still a hot-looking son of a bitch. I just didn't want to be the bitch in question.

CHAPTER SEVEN

*V*anessa and I were prancing around in the pool, warming up for aqua class. She had asked me how my dating was going and I related my creepy encounter with Max. She studied me, eyes wide, shaking her head disapprovingly with accompanying loud tutting noises. I had expected this, of course. She had already set out for me, weeks earlier, her unbreakable rules for dating. And I'd been breaking them all.

'Oh dear, oh dear. *What* were you *thinking?*'

'I know,' I said feebly and pursed my lips. 'I know.'

Vanessa's iron-clad dating rules were:

- Never have sex on the first date.
- Never bring anyone home until you know them well.
- Never pay for anything ('or you'll ruin it for the rest of us!').
- Dine only at top restaurants and drink only champagne ('If they can't afford champagne, they can't afford me').
- Never take public transport, only taxis ('Any man who so much as mentions the tube is out').
- If possible, make them remove all their body hair (Vanessa disliked hairy men, particularly in her own bed, where their stray hairs sullied her Egyptian cotton sheets).

With Max, I didn't know whether she would be more censorious about my having sex on a first date with the Boston Strangler or my picking up the tab for our food and drinks. (Needless to say, Max never did give me the cash, happy for 'mummy' to foot the bill. I was glad he didn't ask me to stump up for a school trip to France, as well.)

Vanessa was dead against the idea of being with much younger men, too, thinking it tasteless and inappropriate. (Well *duh*!) When I'd told her about Little Pup, age 23, she squealed 'He's only a year older than my son!' and said she might be sick in the pool.

She was an intriguing combination of blousy blonde man-eater and Little Goody Two-Shoes. I liked her a lot and liked comparing notes with her on our internet dating adventures. For every man who 'viewed' me online, she was viewed by twenty. Men flocked to her profile in their thousands. I got dozens of winks, she got hundreds. One must never ever underestimate the power of blondeness and bustiness in the sexual imaginings of men. It's not easy for a petite brunette to keep up.

However, we discovered a certain overlap in the men we had been encountering on the site. Jock, for example had been onto her a few times, trying to entice her into a tryst. She had resisted because she didn't like his beard. When I told her about my mindless shag-fest with him, she nodded knowingly and said, 'I'm not at all surprised.'

And then there was BryanG, the 63-year-old engineer from Surrey. After exchanging a few messages, he asked whether we could chat on the phone. He was getting on a bit, but I didn't want to be ageist. He looked fairly presentable, was tall, had his own hair. Educated. Solvent. So I agreed.

I suspected he might be a tad dull but didn't realise quite how dull he was until we had our lengthy conversation one day as I was sitting in the shoe department of Marks and Spencer's at Marble Arch, killing time before an appointment. And when I say *killing* time, I don't use the word lightly. That 25 minutes was bludgeoned to death.

As BryanG droned on about his life and times – encompassing his divorce from his wife of thirty-odd years, the respective professions and family lives of his three married children, his demanding job (which took him to many 'fascinating' parts of the world) and the sad demise of his mum through dementia – I surveyed the nearby pumps, slingbacks and court shoes, desperate for a little light relief.

Still too kindly for my own good, instead of casting him to the four winds without further ado, I said I was very busy for the next fortnight (the usual bullshit) but that maybe we could have a drink sometime after that. He was satisfied with this and said he'd ring again in due course. Great. Another riveting conversation to look forward to.

Vanessa howled with laughter when I told her about all this as we sweltered in the steam room one day after class. She had already been on two dates with BryanG. 'Nothing much happened,' she told me, 'except that we had a snog. It wasn't very nice.'

BryanG had wined and dined her at elegant West End restaurants. He had been boring, she said, but 'the more I drank the easier he was to take'. Anyway, when she informed him after the second date that she didn't wish to take things further, he went a bit funny, claiming he had already 'fallen in love' with her. As Vanessa recounted: 'He said to me "I've invested two expensive dinners in you and paid for your cabs home and now you go and break my heart. I feel I've been used!" So I offered to make dinner for him one night to pay him back but he said no, that would only cause him more pain.'

After hearing this story I resolved that under no circumstances would I meet BryanG for a drink or anything else. What if he fell for me too, after 'investing' in me, only to find that there would be no return on his investment? I didn't need a bleating 63-year-old granddad in my life.

Vanessa knew NiceMan personally, as well. Like me, she'd been on a tame afternoon date with him. Except that instead of going to some common-or-garden establishment as we did, he took her for tea at Fortnum's. Naturally.

'I liked him,' she said. 'But not in *that* way, obviously. He's been having a tough time and I gave him some moral support. We've texted each other a few times since then. Don't think I'll see him again though.'

'I've agreed to go to his place for dinner one night,' I said. 'He says he wants to cook me a meal. Isn't that sweet.'

'A bad idea,' said Vanessa. 'Why did you agree to that?'

'Well, he's a decent guy,' I said. 'I enjoyed his company. And I feel a bit sorry for him. So I told him that although there's no chance of any romantic thing between us, we could just be friends.'

She gave me one of her mildly critical looks. Apparently, I had broken yet another of her golden rules. 'Never tell a man that you can just be friends. Because if they want to have a real relationship with you, they'll keep hoping for more.' She paused before adding meaningfully: 'You must never give them hope.'

The weekend following my misadventure with Max, Little Pup journeyed up from Tooting for another visit. It lifted my heart to see him amble up the drive to my front door, boyish and smiling and straightforward. His hug was like a comfort blanket. Who needed an 'exciting' dude with shades and spiky hair, someone at once 'cool' and 'hot', but whose excitements veered off into the alarming and repugnant?

As before, Pup was gentle and affectionate and attentive. We spent Sunday afternoon in bed, making love, dozing, chatting, laughing. I teased him because we had so few cultural references in common. When 'Sweet Caroline' played on the radio I was amazed to find he had never heard of Neil Diamond. So I set him a little culture test.

'Who was the drummer in the Beatles?'

'Er...pass.'

I groaned. 'Which mega pop star from Wales sang "It's Not Unusual"?' He looked at me blankly, so I sang the first few bars.

'Dunno that one.'

'Christ. Okay, let's get serious. Which American president was shot in 1963?'

He pondered this for a moment, struggling for a name. 'Was it...Nixon?'

I giggled and gave his hair a tug. 'You muppet!' One really couldn't underestimate the failings of the English state school system. But nothing would make me think the less of my Pup.

It occurred to me that, while we had grown close in so many ways, I didn't even know his surname. I hadn't thought to ask. This was one of the peculiarities of internet dating. You could form an almost instant intimacy with a person, but it had no traditional foundation to it, no 'back story'. It just came out of nowhere. Out of the ether. Yet, at its best, it was no less gratifying for that.

Once again we had supper in front of the telly. This time, as we polished off most of a carton of Ben & Jerry's, we watched a DVD of The Graduate. He had actually heard of this sixties classic – wonder of wonders – but never seen it. I told him that the storyline would have a certain relevance to his own life.

When the film was over he remarked that although Mrs Robinson was 'dead sexy', he was glad to say I was much nicer than her. *And* I wasn't married.

I turned to him. 'Okay, here's another question for you. Which famous duo sang "Mrs Robinson", the film's theme song?'

He frowned. 'I'm not playing.'

Sometime in the middle of the night we woke up and I stroked his hair and we started kissing. As he grew roused, he moved on top of me but I told him to wait a moment and reached for the baby oil in my bedside table. Maybe it was time for something different.

Anal sex is one of those love-it-or-hate-it, Marmite-type things. One of my favourite episodes in Sex and the City was on exactly this emotive topic. Demure Charlotte is in a panic because her new boyfriend wants to do anal with her, but she's never done it before and is apprehensive. So the other three girls offer her guidance on anal sex as they all ride together in the back of a cab. Meanwhile the Sikh cab driver, agog at what he's hearing, can't concentrate on his driving.

The analytical Miranda expounds: 'The question is: if he goes up your butt, will he respect you more or respect you less? That's the issue.'

Carrie lights a cigarette and when the driver says there's no smoking in his cab she retorts: 'Sir, we're talking *up the butt*. A cigarette is in order.'

'Front, back, who cares?' says racy Samantha. 'A hole is a hole…and P.S. it's *fabulous*.'

God I loved that show.

That night Pup learned a new trick and as we lay beneath the duvet afterwards, tired and content, I asked him if he had found it exciting.

'If things gets any more exciting,' he murmured, 'I might faint.'

I smiled. He could always make me smile. And with that we drifted off to sleep again.

Sara's Aunt Dolly is down in London, visiting us briefly from her home in Northamptonshire. It is Sunday afternoon and she and I are sitting at my dining table, lingering over glasses of wine after a blow-out lunch. Dolly is a congenial, generous-hearted woman, a divorcee of long standing who hasn't had an easy time of it on the relationship front. Now I am fascinated to learn that she was an early adopter of internet dating, way back in the late-1990s when it was still widely regarded as a questionable fringe activity. 'You had to be a bit madcap to do it then,' says Dolly. 'And I guess I am.'

One of her first online dates was with 'mothball man'. She recalls the episode. 'I was living in Sussex at the time and we met for lunch at a restaurant in Crawley. This ageing guy walks in, reeking of mothballs. He wore jeans that were way too tight, with a pot belly hanging over the top, and an awful old-fashioned jacket that he'd obviously had hanging in his wardrobe for decades and taken out for the occasion. And he had these mashed-up teeth.' She shakes her head in dismay.

'Ugh!' I laugh. 'Could you bear to eat a meal with him?'

'No, I couldn't. I stayed for one drink, trying not to gag on the mothball smell. Then I made a quick getaway.'

'So, a case of creepy in Crawley.'

'Yes! But I had much creepier date than that, a couple of years later.' And she tells me about the fellow she agreed to meet for drinks at a murky backstreet club in Northampton. 'His behaviour was a bit odd from the start. He seemed effeminate. And the more we drank the more weirdly effeminate he became. Then it got very late and we'd both drunk too much, and somehow we ended up back at his place.'

I smile to myself. Dolly and I are more alike than I had realised...

'As he was making us coffee I looked around his kitchen and noticed a shelf full of bottles of pills. Lots of unfamiliar, suspicious-looking stuff. Also anti-depressants. Anyway, a little later we got into bed and then, as we lay there in the dark, it all came out. How he used to be a woman and had already had the sex-change operation but the transformation wasn't yet complete. He was still a bit "she". But he had this new penis and told me he wanted to put it to use with me. Drunk as I was, I knew I ought to get up and leave. But

71

I wasn't in a state to make my way home. So I told him I was really tired and was it okay if we just went to sleep? He didn't answer. And thank god he didn't try anything on with me. I lay in bed nervously, hardly daring to move. And he lay next to me and cried himself to sleep. He was still sleeping when I crept away early in the morning.'

I shudder. How Myra Breckinridge-ish. And I'd thought my Max incident was on the edge.

CHAPTER EIGHT

The evening for the mooted home-cooked dinner at NiceMan's had arrived. He lived in a tiny terraced house in one of those godforsaken, dismal outer suburbs with absolutely nothing to commend it. A place I had managed to avoid during the course of my four decades of living in London. Until now. To make matters worse, it was drizzling. It took me almost an hour to drive there through the soggy north London backwaters.

He had gone to some trouble to prepare a few hot dishes and we sat at a small table in a corner of the small sitting room (everything was small), carefully laid with condiments and folded napkins and a little vase containing a single flower. (Briefly I played with the idea of asking him to take the vase away, as he had done weeks earlier…)

As we ate he inquired about my recent online dating experiences. I regaled him with my Max story – such good copy, I'd be dining out on it for years to come – and he stared at me, horrified. 'How could you bring him home? A stranger! That was such a stupid thing to do.'

Yes, well, perhaps so, but after Vanessa's admonitions and the expected rebuke from Sara which followed ('*Really*, I can see we'll have to lock you in a room for your own protection'), I didn't need another scolding. Especially not from him.

And I knew it wasn't just about concern for my safety. Behind his words was resentment for the fact that I would gleefully take a raunchy bad-boy like Max home with me, but not a Nice Man like him. And what an old story that is in the annals of male-female dynamics.

He told me he was convinced there were lots of dubious men on the dating site, alongside the fishy women. 'The men who don't put a photo up are obviously hiding something. They're probably married. Or on the run. Ha!'

While recalling a deceitful man I'd had dealings with many years earlier, I used the word 'cunt' and his eyes lit up.

'Ah,' he said, 'my favourite word...and my favourite place.' He sounded wistful, like someone without money dreaming of a holiday in the Maldives.

'I think you should give us a chance,' he said. 'We could have a good time together.'

He waited for an answer. I couldn't think of one. Instead I gave him an apologetic, closed-mouth smile.

Later we squeezed up together on his (very small) settee and watched a comedy show on the telly. He *almost* lay his arm around my shoulder but fortunately it didn't quite get there. Then at about ten o'clock I yawned and said I really had to get home. 'It's a long haul back to civilisation,' I said, pretending it was a joke.

He tried to persuade me to stay, but I insisted. On the front doorstep I pecked him on both cheeks and it was with a certain mild relief that I stepped out into the damp night.

He'd been a perfect gent, but I wouldn't be going down this road again (in both senses). Because Vanessa had been right. You can only be 'just friends' with someone who is equally content to be just friends with you. Otherwise you are raising their expectations. And that, in the final analysis, isn't a nice thing to do.

RAVEN: 'I've never been with a black man. I've heard wonderful things, though...'

COOL BLACK STUD AGED 28: 'Ha! That's good. I think you need to be shown what you've been missing out on.'

RAVEN: 'I might be up for that. We should meet and see if we like each other. So what is your considered view of older white women?'

BLACK STUD: 'That they've been missing out by being with white men all their lives. I think the younger generation of white girls are more open (or maybe even prefer) to be with a black man.'

RAVEN: 'Well, I'd like to find out what I've been missing.'

BLACK STUD: 'Want to find out soon?

RAVEN: 'I'm pretty busy for the next few days but I'll see if I can fit you in.'

BLACK STUD: 'Mm...it'll be interesting to see if you can "fit me in". It'll be very exciting, I'm sure.'

RAVEN: 'Hey, I've an idea. I'm at an event in town this evening but it'll probably be over by 8.30. Meet for a drink afterwards?'

BLACK STUD: 'I actually have a date tonight, with a white chick. She's 23 and fun. How about Saturday? We could have the whole day/night together, rather than one rushed evening.'

RAVEN: 'As it happens I've got a date myself on Saturday.'

BLACK STUD: 'With a white guy?'

RAVEN: 'Yup.'

BLACK STUD: 'Can you change it? Black men should always take priority. We'd have an intense day together...a new experience for you, your first black guy.'

RAVEN: 'I can't just blow him out. Not fair.'

BLACK STUD: 'Been trying to control myself from getting too excited thinking about spending time with you. Ditch those white guys. You need it big and you need it black.'

RAVEN: 'Really, you're incorrigible. And just as you're about to go off on a date with some nice kid. I'm shocked!'

But I wasn't shocked in the least. I was growing accustomed to this sex-talk messaging with young guys on the dating site. Most of them cut straight to the chase. I was discovering an army of males in their twenties and early thirties all harbouring fantasies about being with older women. And they had found an easy way of making the fantasies come true. I had been aware that this sort of thing took place on tacky cougar websites, designed specifically for the purpose. But this was an ordinary mainstream site, it was supposed to be about 'dating', not fucking. On their profiles these men were all sweetness and cherry pie, looking to have lovely dates with lovely people and maybe even find that 'crazy little thing called love'. But behind it all there was a lot of hunting going on for the next free shag. Why pay? At this rate hookers would soon be out of business.

There was a 25-year-old in the catering business who caught my eye because, like me, he hailed from Hungary. I sent a jovial hello to this compatriot, who also happened to be easy on the eye. He immediately asked whether I wanted to fix up a 'rendezvous'.

'Sure we can meet up sometime. Although my children are older than you!'

'But you like young guys?'

I thought of Pup. 'Of course.'

'Why do you like them?

'Great bodies and lots of energy, less emotional baggage. Simple!'

'So tell me if I'm wrong but I think you are looking for some fun.'

'Well I'm certainly not looking for a full-time partner right now – been there, done that and got the crummy tee-shirt.'

'If you are looking for some sex…well I can give that to you.'

'Well, you certainly don't waste time. So I guess you're into older women?'

'Yes I am. I find them very attractive and they turn me on much more. You like young bodies. So that's it. If you are looking for the same thing as me, why not?'

'That sounds reasonable. Just as long as you don't expect me to make goulash.'

We exchanged mobile numbers and the next thing I knew he texted me to ask what kind of 'undies' I was wearing. Now it was getting silly. Then he sent a picture showing his washboard stomach and muscular arms. 'Stop showing off,' I replied.

I never heard from him again. My contact with Black Stud fizzled out too, before I had a chance to find out what I'd been 'missing out on'. But that's virtual dating for you – some guys are all jabber and no action. You can be getting on famously with someone, hammering out your hot-blooded messages, hinting at all kinds of future delights, only for the whole shebang to evaporate like snowflakes on the palm of your hand. But as there were always new prospects heaving into view, it really didn't matter.

Not altogether comfortably, I felt as if the process could be changing my attitude towards people. It was slowly commoditising them. And if I commoditised them, surely they did the same to me. It was a worry.

But not a very big one. I was having too much fun. Who would have thought that at sixty I'd be having more down-and-dirty fun than I'd had in any previous decade? In my twenties I was married and starting a family and changing nappies. In my thirties there was more of the same, plus a deteriorating marriage. In my forties I was a single mum toiling in the crucible of Fleet Street in order to survive. And in my fifties I was locked in an unsatisfactory full-time relationship. So, the sexy sixties then. Letting it rip!

It's a cliché, which is why it is so true. All women are enticed by the idea of a man in uniform. Not any uniform, obviously. Not, for example, the uniform of a park attendant. It has to be a *heroic* uniform. So when I got a wink from a tall, dark-haired (albeit thinning-haired) fireman, it got my attention at once. I winked back. He thanked me and our messaging began.

LondonsBurning, aged 39, might have been a hero but his grammar was terrible. He was also a liberal user of the abominable lol. These things offended my literary sensibilities. Nevertheless, I had never been out with a fireman, so this was an opportunity not to be missed.

He was a biker with a Harley Davidson (even more thrilling), so he suggested that as a 'retired biker chick' I might want to get my leathers out of mothballs and hop on the back of his machine.

I had assumed my biking days were definitely over. But perhaps I should think again? I was glad now that my attempts months earlier to sell my panoply of leathers on eBay had been a total flop.

That evening, as he was lounging around at the south London fire station where he was based, we texted each other to arrange a meeting for the following weekend.

'You don't sound too busy,' I said. 'When did you last put out a fire?'

'Today, funnily enough. Nothing major. Small kitchen job. Now we're playing with our hoses. Lol.'

'Sounds kinky.'

'We like to get them out now and then. Does kinda sound naughty.'

'Well I look forward to hearing more naughty firemen's tales at the weekend.'

'U might be shocked.'

'I doubt it.'

I suggested we meet up in my neighbourhood. (Another of Vanessa's diktats: 'Never put yourself out by travelling to some distant part of town for a date; make him come to you.') But LondonsBurning – who was contemplating riding up on his bike – didn't know north London very well and was confused about the route he should take.

'No satnav?' I asked.

'On the Harley? Don't be silly.'

Fair Enough. My ex and I had used a satnav on the Honda Pan European (would have been lost many times without it) but Harley riders were a different breed. They considered themselves *hard*. And on reflection, Dennis Hopper and Peter Fonda wouldn't have been nearly as bad-ass in Easy Rider with little coloured screens in front of them, showing them where to go.

In the end, though, LondonsBurning decided to take the tube so that he could drink. As usual, the venue I chose was The Bells. By now I suspected that the regular bartenders there – two gangly Australian youths and a Czech girl with short dark hair who vaguely resembled Sheena Easton in the eighties – had started to wonder about me, always turning up as I did for an assignation with some new young man. I hoped they wouldn't get the wrong idea…although the *right* idea was possibly not a whole lot better.

My heart sank when I walked in and saw him standing by the bar. I wasn't expecting him to be in full fire-fighting kit, but a little effort would not have gone amiss. Smart casual wear and a pair of decent shoes, perhaps. Or at least some well-fitting jeans and a tucked-in shirt. But LondonsBurning didn't dress to impress. He wore baggy, frayed jeans and a shapeless, un-ironed shirt which hung loosely at his sides. Plus a pair of crappy old trainers. Not quite the image of that valiant heart-throb you would want to heave you over his shoulder and carry you gingerly down a very long ladder. A hero in uniform, maybe, but a hobo out of it.

He was polite and a tad bashful as he bought me a glass of wine and we took our drinks to an outdoor table. Out in the sunlight I noticed that he was looking a little rough, as if he'd been on a bender the night before. And was that a bruise above one eye?

After we sat down he apologised for not being at his best and told me he'd got into a brawl the previous night at a dive in south London where he and his fellow fire-fighters had gone drinking after their shift. He was set upon by an 'evil' East European bouncer and got battered. He lifted up his shirt to reveal an ugly yellow-blue blotch on his left side.

'It's mostly my ego that got hurt, though,' he added with a crestfallen look.

I smiled sympathetically and warmed to him a little. 'I suppose when you're a fire-fighter you're seen as a tough guy and the thugs want to try to bring you down, right?'

He nodded. 'I guess so. If this had happened to me years ago I'd have gone right back there the next night with a couple of mates and we'd have beaten the shit out of that bouncer.' He sipped his beer, looking pensive. 'But now...' A pause. 'Now I think I'll go there in a couple of weeks, on my own, and do the job myself.'

You had to admire him, in a way.

Like me, he had split up with a long-term partner a few months earlier. He had loved her, but they'd had a turbulent relationship and fought all the time. She was more than a decade older than him. Smiling faintly, he said he preferred older ladies, although when an attractive blonde who looked no more than twenty-two walked past, his eyes followed her all the way to her table.

By this stage I knew there would be no second date but I was curious about his background – call it journalistic inquisitiveness – and so I heard all about his career-criminal father who had spent years in jail and who LondonsBurning hadn't seen for a very long time, as well his 'lovely mum' who had slogged away to support him when he was growing up and whom he clearly adored. (Hence his attraction to older women, I surmised, with *no shit, Sherlock* acuity.)

We ordered some food and talked some more and I liked him on a basic level. Rough-cut though he was, he had old-fashioned good manners, pulling my chair out for me, helping me on with my jacket, etc. The kind of escort who would sock a guy on the jaw for making a lewd remark to his date, and that has definite appeal in today's poncy, politically correct world.

When we parted company he said he would like to see me again, 'when he was in better shape', and I suggested we text each other.

He texted late that night: 'I really like you and thanks for being so attentive and understanding. Hope very much to see you again soon.'

I knew that my reply, the next day, wasn't what he wanted to hear. It was along fairly standard lines: enjoyed meeting you, you're a decent guy but we haven't enough in common for us to keep seeing each other, you deserve my honesty, wouldn't want to lead you on, blah blah…'

There were a few more messages, then they petered out. And that was the end of my fireman. Looked like I would be keeping my leathers in mothballs a while longer.

It's Sunday lunch with the family. Big leg of lamb with all the trimmings, the Bordeaux is flowing, the kiddies (aged two and five) are playing with their vegetables before getting bored and scampering off to watch a cartoon.

We've done politics and the fighting in Afghanistan, Boris Johnson's latest antics and plans for a surfing weekend in Cornwall, the kids' erratic night-time sleeping patterns and our favourite moments from Breaking Bad.

Then, in a lull, Older Son (aged 35) asks: 'So Mum, how's it going with the internet dating?'

Sara (a vegetarian) looks up from her veggie-and-nut roast and our eyes meet.

Me (noncommittally): 'Oh yeah, it's been interesting.'

Older Son: 'Been out on a few dates now, I gather from Sara.'

Me, nodding: 'Yes I have, an intriguing variety.' I wonder how much I ought to reveal. Okay, here goes. Because I can't resist a little boast. 'To my amazement I seem to be rather popular with the younger guys!'

Younger Son (aged 29), none too comfortably : 'How *much* younger? I hope they're at least twenty years older than me.'

Me: small awkward laugh.

Younger Son: 'Oh Christ…'

Older Son: '*Mum.*'

Younger Son: 'I don't want to know.'

Me: 'It's just dates. Don't worry. I'm having a nice time. You want me to have a nice time, right? Anyway, last weekend I went out with a fireman. *That* was pretty interesting.'

Older Son (in an approving tone, because as a special constable he's got a lot of time for blokes in the emergency services): 'Yeah? How did that go?'

Me: 'He was perfectly nice to me but I really couldn't see us having – you know – a *relationship* or anything. We agreed to part company.'

Older Son: 'So there was no spark, then?' Cue general laughter.

Younger Son: 'You mean he didn't light your fire, Mum?' More guffaws.

Me (entering into the spirit): 'Maybe I'm just too hot to handle!' And as I down another gulp of wine, I catch Sara smiling at me indulgently.

What would I do without this lot? I say to myself, feeling all cosy inside.

Later, as we're doing the washing-up, Older Son says: 'Just be careful, Mum, with all that dating.'

I don't look at him. 'Sure.'

$\mathcal{A}$ couple of weeks earlier, on one of my regular inspections of the rascals' gallery of men on the dating site – the unending parade of faces with their sometimes bizarre user-names and occasionally original but more often cliché-ridden profile narratives – one face leapt out and instantly captivated me. Charles2013 was a man in his mid-fifties with classic good looks. Swept-back brown hair, hazel eyes, chiselled face and one of those gleaming white smiles common to Hollywood stars. I clicked on his picture and learned that, unsurprisingly, he was an American expat. And by the sound of it, a real high-flyer, looking every bit the business executive it said he was in the box marked 'job description'.

He was in such a different league to the other middle-aged men on the site that I wondered what he was even doing on it. Surely he must already have women hurling themselves at him in the 'real world' – that terrestrial zone that had begun to seem less real to me, in dating terms at least, than cyberspace. For my money it was a no-brainer and I sent him a wink without further ado.

When I received no response I drew the reasonable conclusion that Raven – enthralling though I personally considered her to be – had not triggered an interest. Perhaps

I wasn't glamorous enough for this George Clooney-esque catch. Perhaps he didn't like journalists. I knew it couldn't be my age, because his profile stated that he would consider women up to the age of 58, and I was passing myself off as a mere 54-year-old. Whatever the reason, as the weeks went by without so much as a return wink, Charles 2013 simply receded from my consciousness.

So it was with a gleeful squeal that I found a message from him one morning as I flipped open the trusty laptop.

'Hi "Raven", thank you for looking at my profile and sending a wink. I am flattered! [*He's* flattered?] Sorry for the delay in responding but I've been travelling for the past couple of weeks and just got back to London. I haven't been on this site for a while…'

He explained that he got divorced the previous year from his American wife, who had now returned to the States, and he was attempting to open a new chapter in his life after undergoing a difficult few months adjusting to his changed circumstances. He did a lot of long-haul travelling for his job in a big multi-national company, but London was his base and he loved it here, as did 'so many of us Yanks'. He signed it 'Charles', and added a PS: 'By the way, not all men are rascals!'

He had charm, I thought, and I answered him straight away. 'Hi Charles. I winked at you precisely because you don't seem too rascally. On the contrary! And for your interest, I grew up in the US myself. I'm sure we'll have much in common. Maybe we can meet for a coffee one day?'

But a scant two or three messages later the coffee idea had, between us, morphed into 'drinks', and then 'cocktails'.

I enthused about daiquiris, whilst he favoured martinis. This was going splendidly. Then we exchanged mobile numbers and moved on to texting. 'I'll give you a call tonight,' he wrote. We were rocketing ahead. Graduating to *vocals* already – the final step before an actual meeting, a rendezvous, a *tête-à-tête*. I felt a little thrill.

It was after ten o'clock when my mobile finally rang and I saw Charles's name come up. I'd been dozing in front of an interminable TV documentary about family life in the Middle Ages (tell me about it) and had all but given up on him.

'Sorry it's taken me so long, I've been on the phone to the States for the past hour. Work! With the time difference, I often have to speak to people there late in the evening…'

His voice wasn't as deep and suave as I had imagined it. Not so much George Clooney as Adam Sandler. And he talked a little too fast and too much, the way people do when they are nervous. But the longer we talked the more he slowed down and relaxed.

We covered the usual topics, e.g. our work and past relationships, and somehow ended up discussing TV shows. He said he hardly ever watched TV, except for the news. I told him about my Breaking Bad addiction and terrible habit of picking up Jesse Pinkman's speech patterns, such as putting 'yo' at the end of sentences, which made my sons wince, because 'That doesn't suit an English lady who shops in Waitrose, Mum'. As if I would let that stop me.

'So how do you use that word "yo"?' asked Charles. 'Would you say something like "My bunions are killing me, yo"? Not that I've got bunions.'

I giggled. 'No. You'd say something like [imitating Jesse's voice] *"this shit's the bomb, yo!"*'

'I see...And what does that mean exactly?'

And so we nattered on, and I began to like him a lot. We made a date for Friday evening and I groaned to myself, *oh hell, that's four whole days away...*

On Friday, as our date neared, I applied my make-up carefully. I'd had my hair done that morning, so it was at its optimum. And I put on a sophisticated yet understated outfit: close-fitting black skirt, silk blouse and well-tailored jacket, with black court shoes which looked smart, if a trifle Maggie Thatcher.

I had texted Sara the night before to tell her about this promising new development on the dating front and she wrote back: 'Sounds good but perhaps you can humour me and as a safety precaution text me the details of your meeting place and time, the fellow's name and anything else that might be of use in a police investigation.'

'Ever the optimist, my dear!'

'Yeah, ha ha...except that I'm serious. So I'm expecting a text saying "meeting Mr. American whatsisname in Mayfair" or wherever, and another one after you're back home safe and sound. Okay?'

'Okay, will do. Don't worry!'

Charles and I did meet in Mayfair, as it happened. In the swish bar at Claridge's. He had texted me to say he would get there a few minutes early, 'so that you won't have to wait and have people wonder what an attractive woman is doing alone in a hotel bar'. Exceptionally considerate.

He sent another text moments before I arrived, saying he

was sitting by the window in a dark blue blazer and light blue shirt. As if I wouldn't recognise him!

I walked in, spotted him right away and was struck by his looks; he was even more handsome than in his photos, and exuded a collegiate air. He glanced up from the magazine he was reading, saw me standing at his table and rose to greet me. Then he ordered me a cocktail and we sat back and I thought how lucky I was to be sitting in this glorious bar with this handsome man, sipping my favourite cocktail.

Perhaps it was luck, but then again maybe it was good project management.

We had that conversation – which I now knew to be standard amongst internet daters – in which we compared notes on previous dating experiences, at least the ones that were entertaining. So Charles recounted his headliner, the story of the attractive young brunette who kept sending him messages pleading for a date. He would reply, reiterating that, at 26, she was much younger than his specified age range of 45 to 58, but she refused to give up. Having wheedled his mobile number out of him, she proceeded to send him fetching pictures of herself. 'Nothing improper,' Charles pointed out, 'just pictures of her looking pretty in the garden, in the kitchen, at her desk, all over the place. In the end, well, you know how weak men are. I gave in and agreed to have a drink with her.'

They arranged to meet before the main entrance at Selfridges, where Charles was standing at the allotted hour, waiting for her to turn up. After bombarding him with so many photos of herself, he was sure he would recognise her. But when he heard his name called out and swung around, he had no idea who the enormously fat woman standing next to him was. That was when it dawned on him that all her photos had been head and shoulders shots.

'My God,' said Charles, 'she had a backside the size of this table.' And he tapped the table at which we were sitting. I shook my head in amazement. Then I laughed merrily, with the shameless *Schadenfreude* that a sixty-year-old woman who wears size 10 would naturally feel at hearing such a tale.

His eyes sparkled in the evening sunlight that beamed on him through the window, and he kept them on me while taking another sip of his martini. 'When I saw *you* standing there, on the other hand, my first thought was: Wow, who's she? I'll tell her I'm waiting for somebody but maybe we can hook up later.'

I laughed again. 'Schmoozer.'

He told me about another of his dating flops, with a divorcee in her forties, a mother of two young children. 'I liked her but kept thinking: would she expect me to put her kids through school? I can't take on that sort of responsibility.'

That could have been me, twenty years earlier. The divorced mum with a challenging domestic set-up was a tough gig for any prospective suitor, as I understood only too well. But for me that problem was ancient history. This was now. And the good news was that, in the contest for Charles's affections, so far I was beating the competition hands down.

Time for honesty. 'I'm older than you think, Charles.'

'Really?'

I nodded. 'Sixty,' I said with a mock dramatic flourish. Then I leaned forward, elbows on the table. 'Do you mind?'

When he replied, 'Not at all,' I eased back into my chair.

After we'd had three cocktails apiece and the booze had begun to go my head, I suggested we go someplace for a bite to eat. So we headed off down the road to a local Italian restaurant I knew, where we had pasta and a bottle of full-bodied red, and by now I was well and truly merry. But Charles wasn't done yet.

He called the waiter over and ordered two Limoncellos and I thought *uh-oh*. The last time I had indulged in this deceptively potent Italian liqueur, on a Tuscan holiday, I'd woken up feeling as if King Kong were banging on my head. The trouble was I rather liked the stuff and had no trouble downing it. As soon as I'd finished the last lethal drop, Charles asked the waiter for two more of the sticky yellow snifters.

I had been matching Charles drink for drink, although I was five foot four and he was six foot two. Naturally he would be the one to stay sober and I the one to get tipsy and misbehave. I hadn't planned to. In fact I had determined to follow Vanessa's rules to the letter and be thoroughly lady-like and respectable. No inviting him home, no sex on the first date.

That was the plan. But looking across the table at his handsome face, a face I'd been wanting to kiss all evening, and emboldened by the Limoncellos, I opened my mouth and without further ado took the sophisticated, yet under-stated approach: 'Why don't you take me home and fuck my brains out?'

His eyes met mine and I didn't note, through the boozy fug, whether or not he smiled or showed any surprise. I only heard three little words: 'I'd love to.'

I had little recollection afterwards of how we got to my house, only a dim sense of having ridden up and down some tube escalators (another transgression for which Vanessa would no doubt give me the tut-tut treatment). Then all of a sudden I found myself unlocking the door and climbing up the stairs and dropping down onto my bed, with Charles gently pulling off my shoes.

I wriggled out of my clothes, crawled under the duvet and was easing into a heavy sleep when I gasped and sat up abruptly. 'My mobile, my mobile,' I mumbled. 'Have to text Sara. Have to tell her I'm okay.' The next thing I knew Charles was handing me my phone. God knows how I sent a coherent text in my woolly state, and with faultless spelling and punctuation, to boot. Just goes to show how the technology has now seeped right into our brain cells. Is that good? I don't know. But all that mattered was that I performed my duty to my daughter-in-law, and with that I flopped back down on the pillow and was over and out.

Sometime in the middle of the night I was awake again, with Charles lying beside me. I reached over and touched his cheek, and he turned to me. My fuzziness was gone. There was just enough light for me to make out his face; he was peering down at me and I thought he was smiling. 'You all right?' he asked and I answered with a small 'Mm-hm'.

A little later, as he made love to me slowly and gently, I cried for a brief moment – just a single gasp and a couple of warm tears which wet my face – and had no idea why.

It was mid-morning and we were still in bed, talking, our arms around each other, as my hangover gradually slipped away. He described to me the bachelor apartment he bought after his divorce, in a mansion block in Marylebone. 'It's smaller than the place I had with my wife, but it's got everything I want. You'll have to come over and see it soon.'

For my part, I mused on the matter of my half-owned house and when I might finally sell and move on to...who knew where? With a sigh I said, 'I'm in limbo.'

Charles didn't 'do breakfast', so after getting dressed and downing a large orange juice, he was ready for me to drive him down to the tube station. As he glanced out the window at the humdrum 1930s suburban houses along the way, he said casually, 'You should make your age on the site even lower, to 49. You could easily pull it off. And you'd have an even better hit rate.'

I found his remark vaguely upsetting. Not the bit about my age, obviously. But that he considered it a good idea for me to be dating more – and not fewer – men.

Back home I finally thought to check my mobile and found a text from Sara. 'Is he second date material, then?'

'Definitely. Think I'll be seeing him again soon.'

'So, not too well-behaved not to have sex appeal. Sounds good!'

During my next aqua class, two days later, I swam up to Vanessa, and yelling to be heard above the thumping Abba remix, eagerly told her about the date with 'my Yank', Charles2013.

She seemed to be thinking hard, as we leapt to left and right in unison. 'Does he travel a lot, some sort of businessman, lives in...Marylebone?' she called out.

'Yes! How do you know?'

'He messaged me not long ago. But I didn't respond.' I threw her a curious look. 'Tell you about it later, darling!' she said as she splashed off through the churning water.

Reconvening in the steam room after class, Vanessa told me that she had felt there was something dubious about Charles, which was why she ignored his attempt to establish contact with her.

'Dubious in what way?'

'Dunno. Maybe it's just me, maybe he's really fine. But he's not my type. Anyway, you like him, so go for it.'

'Yes I do like him. *And* he's great in bed.' I added in a more weighty tone, 'He's the first guy I've met on that site who is proper relationship material.'

She tilted her head at me. 'I thought you were only after a good time?'

I turned to Vanessa and shrugged. 'Hmm. Not sure.' It was true that according to my profile I wasn't in search of a long-term relationship (the oft-cited yet elusive LTR), but would any woman turn one away, should a promising prospect unexpectedly crop up?

Then with a guffaw she regaled me with her own latest dating antics. She had been naughty and broken her own rules. 'That guy Dennis who'd been messaging me for ages – I told you about him, right? He's the nice-looking 50-year-old sales manager – well I finally gave in and said he could take me out. We had four bottles of champagne and were getting on like a house on fire, so I let him take me home and he came in and we started snogging. He was a great kisser. And I thought, he's bloody sexy, so when he said he wanted to have sex, I said yeah why not, and off we went to the bedroom.' She took a breather for effect, and as the sweat dripped off our heads, I wondered what the others in the steam room – a muscular young man and two dumpy middle-aged Indian women – were making of her story.

'So anyway,' she went on, 'he took off all his clothes and his body was completely covered in *grey hair*…and I took one look and said "Ugh! Put your clothes back on, I'm not having *that* in my bed!" It was disgusting. I made him get dressed again and sent him packing. I mean – *what the fuck* – I'm not going to bed with a werewolf!'

Vanessa was such a scream.

Returning to the subject of Charles, she offered to play the little game that she sometimes indulged in with another friend of hers, who also subscribed to our dating site, whenever one of them started seeing a man they liked. They would 'put him to the test'.

If it looked as though a relationship might be forming for either of them, the other would send a wink or message to the man involved, to see how he responded to temptation. Did he express an interest or politely refuse because he had 'already found someone'? Now Vanessa said: 'If you like I can test your Yank to find out if he's still interested in me. And I'll ask him if he's met anyone special on the site, see what he says.'

But I said no. I didn't think I wanted to know how he would respond to temptation. Following my fiasco with SuperA, I knew I mustn't mind how much time any man was spending on the site, winking and flirting, or how many dates he was going on with others. But with Charles I suspected I *would* mind, too much.

Besides Charles there was only one other I cared about and that was Pup. I was very fond of him and believed it to be reciprocated. There was a bond between us. But of course that was different. That was never going to be a 'proper relationship'. That (as Nick Hornby would have said) was about a boy.

CHAPTER TEN

While getting ready for my second date with Charles (we were dining out at a hip Vietnamese restaurant near me), I imagined introducing him to my sons and considered how they would get on. They could hardly fail to be impressed by his many attributes. I pictured us all sitting around a dinner table, bantering, growing familiar, forming bonds. And I knew Charles would just love my smart, funny, attractive sons. He didn't have children of his own. Perhaps mine would add a valuable dimension to his life which was missing.

Of course I realised I was jumping the gun – this was only our second date, after all – but I had spent a lifetime being impetuous and I wasn't about to change now.

As I watched him amble across the street from the tube station to my car, I was struck all over again by his classic American good looks, and felt a little stab of gratification that he should be attracted to *me*. It was a warm, sunny evening in early June, he wore an open-necked shirt and I wore a fetching silk frock, we both had our shades on, and as we roared off in the direction of West Hampstead I thought we made a fine-looking pair.

Over dinner our relaxed conversation flowed effortlessly, as we were surrounded by tablefuls of animated Londoners, mostly young, enjoying the weather outside, the ambience inside, the exotic fare. This was unassuming West Hampstead at its most seductive and we were part of it all, and if I had thought about it – which I didn't – I would have realised that it was one of 'those moments' when you are blissfully, stupidly, totally happy.

Back at my place afterwards he handed me the stiff paper bag he'd brought with him from town. 'Something for you,' he said.

It contained a bottle of Limoncello, with a card which read: 'Thank you for accelerating matters between us by making your true intentions known during the course of our first date...and thank you to the makers of Limoncello, for their part in the acceleration!'

I laughed and stood on my toes to give him a kiss.

That night in bed we had the 'orgasm conversation'. (I had been through this a few times already, with others.) Charles had been applying himself with expertise and much careful attention to the chief erogenous area, but as I'd been expecting, sensuous and highly pleasurable though it all was, 'it' didn't happen. That was because, for me, orgasms had become a very tricky number. Since splitting up with my partner, no one else seemed capable of making it happen for me. Not even dear Little Pup, who, for one so young, was surprisingly adept at the orals. Possibly it was all to do with what was inside my head...or *not* inside my head, as the case may be.

That night, more than anything, I wanted Charles to be able to perform magic. I wanted him to be the one to break through the barrier. But he couldn't. He was persistent and would have carried on, slaving away at the coalface, but I didn't want him to get bored. People in the 21st century didn't generally have much of an attention span.

'Sorry,' I mumbled, as I held his shoulders and pulled him up towards me. I tried to explain. 'The crazy thing is, it can only happen with my vibrator these days. Dunno why...' But the truth was that even my trusty vibrator had been taking an age to pull it off. Not five or ten minutes like in earlier times. But half an hour, forty-five minutes. Ridiculous! The batteries didn't last long, I can tell you.

What had caused this physiological change in me? I worried about it. If it went on like this, could I perhaps lose the ability to climax altogether? *Christ*, could I be developing the dreaded 'Wendy syndrome'?

Wendy had been a friend of mine since our kids were in nursery school together, and over the decades we had had many a heartfelt chinwag about the great issues of life: love and relationships, marriage and divorce, sex and no sex. The usual things women talk about when their menfolk aren't there. And one of Wendy's defining characteristics was that she had never had an orgasm, and I mean *never*. She had absolutely no idea what an orgasm was like, and yet was utterly unbothered by the fact that this most basic of life's sensations had somehow passed her by.

She was with her husband Frank for more than thirty years, they had virtually been childhood sweethearts, and were in many ways a devoted couple. As Wendy often said: 'We're best friends.' Frank was tall and well-built and attractive, with one of those craggy, lived-in faces. He gave Wendy a good life, two great kids, big house and annual holidays on the Med. But he could never give her an orgasm. She shrugged it off.

I was the reverse. I was twenty-one when I discovered this particular pleasure – a late start, but then there was no stopping me. In my early twenties I would sometimes even pop into the ladies' room at work for a quick DIY job during office hours. Five minutes and back to my desk, feeling well pleased with things. No problem.

But that was long, long ago. Now, at sixty, I was becoming orgasmically deprived. It was getting to be an ever rarer occurrence. And such hard work. I was even starting to wonder, Wendy-like, whether the orgasm wasn't perhaps an overrated biological function. Which was ironic in the extreme, because it was at precisely this time that Wendy, at long last, had her first orgasm, aged 61.

Poor Frank had been killed in a road accident and Wendy was comforted by an old family friend, who was himself single again following his break-up with his partner. Before too long Wendy and Richard had become inseparable, middle-aged lovebirds looking forward to a future together. I had never met Richard but Wendy told me all about him when she came over for supper one evening.

'I finally get it,' she said, grinning. 'God, I *finally* get what it's all about. I'm having the best sex of my life. Two, *three* orgasms a night.'

I gawped at her in awe. From plenty of nuthin' to Woody Allen's orgasmatron, virtually overnight. Even in my heyday I could never manage more than one per session. 'How on earth did it happen?' I was dying to find out the secret recipe.

'Richard is just incredible, the things he can do. He makes me feel things I'd never felt before and it's all so *exciting*.'

Naturally, I was keen to meet this genius of the bedroom arts. And a couple of weeks later I did, when he and Wendy held a barbecue party in her garden and invited me along.

I don't know what I had been subconsciously expecting – some kind of rugged Marlboro man, perhaps, with a sexy glint in his eye – but I could scarcely believe it when this diminutive, fusty-looking man came hobbling towards me bearing a jug of Pimm's. With his thick glasses, receding hairline and ill-shaven chops, he could have been a retired provincial librarian, or perhaps a member of the planning committee in some rundown seaside town. And what was with the funny walk?

But there you have it. This unlikely candidate was Wendy's love god. And while I wouldn't want a weaselly little fellow like that tampering with my own privates, thanks to him Wendy was at long last firing on all cylinders. And I was delighted for her.

Towards the end of my second date with Charles, in the morning, just before we got out of bed and returned to our respective day jobs, he said something I didn't want to hear: 'I'm going to be really busy for a while. Colleagues coming from the States, lots of meetings, business dinners. Just give me a couple of weeks, okay? Then we can be together again.'

Uneasy echoes of SuperA. But I refused to let that concern me. Because Charles wasn't anything like SuperA. Charles actually seemed to care about me. He had thanked the makers of Limoncello for helping to accelerate matters between us, and by matters he clearly meant our *relationship*. Because that was what this felt like – the blossoming of what could be a real relationship. So I just tightened my arms around his neck and said it was a shame. Two weeks! But that was all right, and we would have to think of something really nice to do on our next date.

'Do you like the theatre?' I asked.

'Sure. We'll do something like that.'

Perhaps I imagined it, but I thought I caught a slightly hesitant note in his voice.

One day I received a wink and message from Scotland. Andy was 28 and worked for a publishing company in Edinburgh. His pictures showed a studious-looking young man in glasses. Open, guileless face, pleasant smile.

Andy: Hi. I know I'm a lot younger and far away. But I like the way you look. I hope my wink didn't offend?

Me: Not at all. You look rather sweet yourself. And I like younger men.

Andy: And I like older women.

Me: Do you wear a kilt?

Andy: Only if you want me to.

Andy was shy and inexperienced with women. He needed someone who had been around the block to take him in hand and give him a bit of self-confidence. 'You're very nice,' he wrote, and a few messages later he wasn't too shy to suggest that he would make a good toy boy.

'Ah, well that depends, Andy. Are you planning to vote for Scottish independence?'

'No, but I have a cute Scottish accent.'

'Can I hear it? Call me.'

But Andy was too bashful for that.

After some of my recent dating experiences, his boyishness was refreshing. He got straight to the point, though. 'I think you could help me a lot. Do you think we would be good in bed together? I'll bet you could teach me a thing or two!'

I tried to explain that it was impossible to predict such a thing until we had actually met and seen whether we hit it off. 'We'd have to have a drink and a bite to eat and chat about publishing and Robbie Burns and haggis for a while first. Then we'd know whether or not we fancied each other.'

Of course, his living 400 miles away was an obstacle to any such agenda, and that was fine with me.

'Anyway Andy, I don't see you as a toy boy. That's just a plaything. It seems to me you are worth more than that.'

'You are lovely.'

'You mean for a Sassenach?'

He wanted to come down to London and spend a weekend with me, but I wasn't up for that. Not only because of what had begun with Charles. In any case, I would never commit myself to spending an entire weekend with some fellow I had never clapped eyes on, not even one as sweet and shy as Andy. So I rejected this idea.

'Sorry, Andy. I assume you're not an axe-murderer, but even so!'

'Okay.' And with that single crestfallen word he disappeared off the radar. I would have liked to help the guy out, honestly I would, but he'd started to make me feel as if I were some sort of unpaid social worker with a brief to assist the sexually disadvantaged.

After the Scotsman came the Irishman. (I know, it was beginning to sound like a comedy routine.) But while Andy had been a gentle naïf, Ryan was a flagrant Casanova, crude, over-heated and extraordinarily confident of his desirability as far as the opposite sex was concerned. He was 35, but despite stating on his profile that his 'ideal date' was aged 25 to 35, he told me he much preferred 'a mature woman who knows what she wants'. Ryan was tall and brawny, and admittedly highly appetising with his dark hair and bright blue eyes. His charms drew me in, as he must have guessed they would.

RYAN: Fancy some fun? How about a drink somewhere near yours and if we click we go back and explore each other in private. Lying in bed naked now, thinking about it.

ME (amused): You're in a hurry.

RYAN: Yes I am! What's your dress and cup size?

ME (slightly irritated but still enjoying the game): Now you're getting tacky. Listen, I'm slim, no huge boobs, so if you're looking for some blow-up doll you've come to the wrong place.

RYAN: No, not at all. Want a real woman who loves sex and has a brain.

ME: You can tick both boxes.

RYAN: When we go back to yours I will give you a sensual massage first.

ME: That sounds nice. And have you got a cute Irish accent?

RYAN: No, but I can turn it on. What turns you on, apart from
    the accent?

And so we played on. Ryan was a thrilling prospect, in the
way that hang-gliding might be for someone who has never
been. I didn't think I could turn him down. I didn't want to.
He was dead sexy. So after a little persuasion I agreed to let
him come over late that night, after the 'gig' he was attending
with a mate.

I could hardly believe it when during the intermission at
whatever concert he was at, he texted to inquire whether I
had a 'clean ironed shirt' for him, as he needed it for work
the following morning.

'Yeah, sure,' I replied. 'And should I polish your shoes as
well?'

But he was insistent about the shirt and so, after a little
further beefing about it, I went off to search for one and
found an old striped shirt of my ex's, which I had occasionally worn while mooching about the house. It was clean but
creased, so I grudgingly got out the iron and the board and
ironed the damn shirt, wondering all the while what Vanessa
would say about my performing this servile act, not to
mention the entire feminist sisterhood. Then I sat down to
watch some telly until Ryan arrived; he told me he would be
at my place by 11 o'clock.

But the Irish stud, God's gift to the fairer sex, never showed
up or got in touch. When I tried to call him, his mobile was on
voicemail. I finally trudged off to bed just before midnight,
tired, depressed, angry and humiliated. I promised myself I
would never do anything like that again and I was *serious*.

The last thing I saw that night before switching off my bedside light was the striped shirt hanging, beautifully pressed, on my wardrobe door. Asshole, I thought.

I decided to consign Ryan to the dating dustbin. Rather than take issue with his inexcusable behaviour, I preferred simply to forget him. He wasn't worth the time it took to send a furious message. But he would not be forgotten. The following afternoon my mobile tinkled with the arrival of a contrite message.

RYAN: Hey sorry about last night. Phone died. No way to contact you. Can I come and make it up to you tonight?

ME: Oh really. Why should I believe that? I won't be jerked around and I know what shits most men are.

RYAN: No, honest. My iPhone5 battery is terrible.

ME: And it took you all day to let me know?

RYAN: Been in meetings all day at work. [I had no idea what his vague 'management' job description entailed and neither did I care.]

ME (softening slightly): So what are you proposing?

RYAN: I can come over tonight at 8. Okay? I owe you a full body massage…followed by passionate sex.

ME: Better make it super-passionate then.

RYAN: Don't worry. I will want to rip your clothes off as soon as I see you. [How could he be so sure? I wondered.]

ME (totally forgetting my promise to myself of the night before): Well, then you'd better charge your phone. Now.

Early that evening I took a long scented bath and carefully went through my whole grooming routine, then deliberated over what to wear, finally choosing a pair of figure-hugging black trousers and sleeveless lacy top. I laid the clothes out on my bed and started to work on my hair, which could take a fair bit of taming.

He had said he would call before setting off, in order to confirm directions to my house, so when it got to 7.30 and I still hadn't heard anything I texted him, a little uneasily: 'Helloooo. What's happening?' I got a return message a moment later.

RYAN: Send me a photo of you.

ME: Sorry? You want me to audition?

RYAN: Want to see what you look like.

ME (crossly): I don't do naked pics and you already know what I look like with clothes on. Should we just say you're a twat and call the whole thing off?

RYAN: Take a photo now.

ME (even crosser): Fuck off. I don't need to demean myself for anyone.

RYAN: Send a classy pic in your lingerie and I'll be there.

ME: How's about a pic of you in Y-fronts? Got a six-pack? How many inches are you?

RYAN: You send a lingerie pic first.

ME: Otherwise you're not coming?

ME AGAIN (after receiving no reply for several minutes): Right, I'm done messing around. You need to grow up. Bye.

I couldn't believe I had wasted hours, once again, on that Irish lecher. He was 35, going on 15. I could just picture him in another ten years, still manning his dodgy stall on the dating site, luring in unsuspecting females and then setting them up with his deceitful blarney and adolescent demands for lingerie shots.

But maybe that's what I had coming, for not waiting calmly and patiently for Charles to re-emerge from his business exec's purdah. Almost three weeks had passed since our last, highly promising tryst, during which we had exchanged only the odd brief 'how are you' text. I was eager to be with him again. Where was he already?

CHAPTER ELEVEN

*A*nd where was I? Ah yes, the Scotsman, the Irishman and then came the Englishman, whom I will call George, naturally.

George, who was 48, so hated his job as a property lawyer that he gave up the law, but then promptly forgot to find some other means of earning his daily crust. So when we met he had been unemployed for a couple of years and had by now possibly become unemployable, because he appeared to be doing nothing with his life besides hanging about on the dating site day and night, gazing at women's photos, checking out their profiles and sending random winks and messages to the ones that caught his horny eye.

I fell into this net one evening when George messaged to say he found me 'enticing' and asking whether I had any plans for that evening. He looked fairly presentable and his profile, if somewhat awkwardly and self-consciously composed, seemed sane at least.

ME: This evening? Boy, you move fast. And would it be a drink and conversation you are after, or something more intimate? I am not one of those desperate older women, you know, gagging for a shagging.

GEORGE: That would be entirely up to you. I'm not the type to pressurise a woman into anything.

ME: Yes, I am sure you are well-behaved. But I've been getting overt come-ons from guys younger than my sons who only want the one thing and even before they've met me, for Pete's sake.

GEORGE: All men want the one thing. It's just that some of us are more honest about it than others. Lots of men will feed you the flannel and bullshit which they think you want to hear. So…fancy meeting up?

ME: Well, first of all I would have to take a bath, wash my hair, decide what to wear. That would take us up to 8.30 at least.

GEORGE: Okay, let's meet at nine.

I always felt I had Sara sitting on my shoulder at times like that, and she would now doubtless be jumping up and down. *Don't do it!* But George called me on the mobile and we talked in a sensible, grown-up fashion, he was quietly-spoken and articulate and, what the hell, I wasn't doing anything that evening. So I invited him over for a drink.

As he lived in Islington, he drove across London from east to west and through Regent's Park, arriving at my place on the dot with a bottle of wine. We sat down on the sofa, sipped our drinks and conversed about our lives, as the light summer breeze flowed in from the garden through the French doors, and George was, to all intents and purposes, like some old-fashioned 'gentleman caller' in a play by Tennessee Williams. Very genteel, we were.

But the longer we talked the more morose George grew. It was clear that he hated himself. He told me he had never married, never had kids and never had a relationship which lasted more than a year or two. Besides all that, he said he had failed to find his true vocation, was a layabout and embarrassment to his family and friends, and had put on weight and was now fat. This last self-accusation was patently absurd, as he was actually quite trim.

He appeared to be a fundamentally decent guy and I felt sorry about his being carried away on this tidal wave of self-loathing. 'I'm a failure and a coward,' he declared gloomily. I didn't want to agree with him, yet I knew that he would scornfully wave aside any of the standard platitudes usually wheeled out to buck people up in such situations. Because the key thing about George was that he was extremely intelligent and you couldn't bluff him with banalities. Just about the only thing he seemed proud of was the fact that, as a kid from an ordinary small-town family who had attended a run-of-the-mill comprehensive, he had won a scholarship to Oxford and got a first-class law degree. He interested me.

'Just out of curiosity, George, without a job, what do you do for money?'

'Live off savings.'

'What about when your savings run out?'

'I'll sell my house.'

'Yeah, and then what?

'I dunno.' He shrugged. 'Something will happen.'

He was scathing about the women he had met through the dating site: 'Boring secretaries, mostly, who take holidays in Torremolinos.' He had also tried the personal ads columns in some of the newspapers. 'First I tried the Guardian. Had a few dates. It was like going out with Swampy. Women in ugly sandals with pierced noses, who belonged up a tree. So I moved on to the Times, where the women looked more respectable but all thought they should be married to a cabinet minister. They had no time for me, obviously an abject failure.'

He seemed so paralysed with hopelessness and the expression on his face was so despondent that my heart went out to the guy.

Fatal move. The next thing I knew we were heading upstairs for the act of human compassion commonly known as a mercy fuck.

George wasn't such a pessimist, however, that he did not come prepared with a supply of condoms. Our coupling was an intense but mechanical affair, during the course of which a baffling number of condoms were put on and taken off, at odd moments. The whole process didn't convince me that there should be a follow-up.

Later, as I ushered him out the front door, I gave his cheek a playful pinch. 'Try not to beat yourself up, George. It's a real downer for other people and you'll never get a girlfriend that way.'

'I'm a loser.'

'You will be if you keep telling yourself that. Just find something you like doing and do it.'

'Easy for you to say.'

'Yes it is. Because it's true. And meanwhile find somebody nice to date. It shouldn't be so difficult online.'

He threw me a doleful look as he strode off to his car. 'Oh yeah? Try being a man.'

'I'd love to!' I called after him. 'It's a man's world, in case you haven't heard!'

But I'm not sure I really believed that.

Every few days I had noticed that Charles was active on the dating site. Of course I would never mention this to him. I wouldn't want him to think I noticed, or cared. I did care, needless to say. But I knew the worst thing I could do was give the impression I was snooping on him. But anyway, as a well-behaved man he was probably only logging on to the site, every so often, to send polite replies to the many ladies understandably captivated by his charms, the army of winkers and messagers. Right?

Meanwhile I carried on trucking with my own dating activities, for good or ill, so I was hardly in a position to gripe about *his* doings. Something had happened between Charles and me, of that I was certain. He just needed time to realise that fully and take the next step. After all, he was a man, and men required careful, patient handling or they would take fright like skittish horses and gallop off into the dusty distance.

At this point an affable old geezer took a fancy to me, clearly beguiled by the crafty reference on my profile to my former biker chick days. 'Grab your leathers, put your helmet on, and meet me down the Ace Cafe for a fry-up. You're only young once!' wrote the 65-year-old DanBoy, retired oil rig worker and as-yet-unretired biker dude. When I sent an appreciative response, he wrote: 'You're unique!! Most people on here wouldn't go within a mile of a bike, let alone a biker who plays guitar in a rock band.' (Rock music was another of his passions, and I admit that appealed to me. He might be getting on a bit, I told myself, but DanBoy knows how to have a good time.) It also occurred to me that, while it hadn't worked out with the Harley-riding LondonsBurning, I might yet hop back on a pillion with this new contender.

There was a downside to DanBoy, however. In addition to the photos of him performing with his fellow old-fart rockers, and the ones showing him astride his Honda Blackbird, his profile displayed a few snaps showing a boring caravan sitting by itself on a bleak, windswept landscape. What was that all about? I wondered. And I soon found out.

'I keep a caravan on the north Norfolk coast,' he informed me, 'and love to go there for long spells to enjoy the peace and beautiful scenery.'

This was off-putting indeed. I recalled my married days, decades earlier, when we owned a weekend cottage in a small north Norfolk village. A worryingly remote part of the country, where you were considered irredeemably foreign if you didn't have five generations of ancestors buried in the village graveyard. Even the denizens of the neighbouring village, five miles down the road, were seen as strangers and treated warily. These in-bred locals spoke in a flat, dull accent and definitely could have done with a dose of bright lights, big city, to jolt them out of their rural torpor.

And then there were the scurrying mice in the thatched roof...

At the end of every Norfolk weekend, as we hit the road back to London, my heart lifted with hope and joy.

Should I tell DanBoy any of this?

He called me one evening and we had a long chat, although he did the lion's share of the talking. For the first fifteen minutes I heard about the devastating breakdown of his first marriage, due to the adultery perpetrated by his heartless wife, and how neither he nor his children ever forgave her. That was bad enough. Then came the second fifteen minutes, during which DanBoy shared with me the trauma of his Wife Number Two's intolerable behaviour towards him, exacerbated by her drink problem. In the end she ran off, too, shattering once more his faith in womankind. And all this time I was thinking: where's the fun, dude?

Still, I made all the right sympathetic noises, and by the end of our elongated conversation we had planned our first date. On the following Saturday evening, three days hence, he would drive into London from his home in Hertfordshire and we would dine at a favourite haunt of mine, a Chinese restaurant near Hampstead. I booked a table.

But DanBoy texted me on the Friday: 'Hi. Hope you don't mind but as this rare fine weather is due to last into the weekend I have decided to make the most of it and take my grandchildren away to the caravan. Perhaps we can catch up during next week. Dan x.'

I was slightly miffed at being so easily blown out. There was my plan for Saturday evening gone. Now what would I do? It would have been worse, of course, had he suggested taking *me* to the caravan for the weekend. But even so. If anyone was going to do blowing out, I would have preferred to do it myself.

The following week came and went, and the week after that. I didn't hear from DanBoy again and never contacted him to find out what had put the old buffer off. Another mystery, like that French freak, Édouard. So once again, there would be no hot-shot biking for me. Nor any bopping along to his rock band's rendition of Long Tall Sally at some small-town garden fête. But I didn't care much. As I took one last look around his photo gallery and gazed at the snaps of his beloved caravan stranded in that East Anglian desolation, I imagined my own miserable face peering out through one of its rain-splattered windows. *Help! Get me out of here!*

But with one bound I'd been set free.

After this episode I adopted a harder edge. No longer would I unfailingly respond in kindly mode to every message received, no matter how lamentable the sender. 'Thank you for your interest, I do appreciate it…' From now on I would just ignore the ones that didn't immediately grab me. Too dull? Not good-looking enough? Can't spell? Next!

Would this new-style Raven have driven through the rain all the way up to the dreary north London hinterland to sit with NiceMan in a tiny sitting room, smiling uncomfortably whilst he attempts to cajole her into a relationship? No, I fear this Raven would have cut NiceMan off at the knees very early on, with no chance at all of 'face time'.

I am having dinner at one of my trendy local eateries with my friend Francine, who is three years younger than me. She runs her own business and is one of those women who is successful and tough and powerful in her professional life but, as she readily admits, hopeless in her relationships with men. She has had three long-term relationships and they have all ended in acrimony. Talk about rascals. These men abused her, cheated on her, lied to her and took her money. She always manages somehow to pick a rotter, who then proceeds to trample all over her life. I haven't seen her since the last of these relationships ended a few months earlier, and Francine tells me she is through with being a victim. It seems she has discovered her inner Boadicea.

'Harry used to make me so depressed,' she says, and her expertly made-up face and expensive coiffure ooze glamour in the warm light of the candle on our table. Her perfume wafts over to me. 'In the office I am always in charge, everyone respects me, I'm happy with myself and my achievements. But with Harry, as soon as I walked through the door at home I felt useless. I did everything I could think of to please him, but nothing ever did. When he told me I was too fat I went on a diet. I bloody starved myself for that man and lost twelve pounds and he didn't even notice.'

'He was jealous of you, Franny,' I say as I munch my rocket salad, 'because you are way more successful than he is.'

She nods thoughtfully. Then her eyes light up and she announces: 'Anyway, I'm free now! And I'm not on a diet any more! From now on no one can tell me what to eat, what not to eat. The day after Harry and I split up I went food shopping and I went crazy in the supermarket, charging up and down the aisles, tossing all my favourite things into the trolley – stuff I hadn't bought in years because *Harry* didn't approve.'

'Oh yeah? Like what?'

'Walnut Whips!'

I laugh and then she laughs and I give her arm a squeeze.

Then Francine asks about my internet dating and I give her a summary of the story so far.

'I hope you're being careful,' she says.

'Well, sure, I try to be. Pretty much.' I smile at her feebly. 'Sara wants me to text her with the name, rank and serial number of every bloke I have a drink with. Ha ha!'

'I don't mean that. I mean I hope you're using protection.'

'Oh.' We are going to have the condom conversation.

'Listen, a friend of mine didn't use protection and got chlamydia recently. It put a real damper on her sex life. And she should have known better. She's almost seventy.'

'Rock and roll!' I laugh.

'It isn't a joke.'

'No, no. I know. Don't worry, I'm being careful.'

But that isn't strictly true. I always *aim* to be careful. But as with waiting for the green light before crossing a road, I'm not dogmatic about it. Women of my age, who can no longer get pregnant, tend to stop thinking about things like condoms and coils and caps. And that is a liberation, just as the Pill was a liberation for us when we were young and fertile. So in the heat of the moment, I have at times found it all too easy to forget the exhortations (from Sara, Vanessa, et al.) to be 'careful'.

But I had read the newspaper articles about the rise in STDs amongst the older generations, who were living longer and fitter lives and apparently still going at it like rabbits, with nary a care in the world. So I did see the *potential* for coming unstuck.

And with that in mind, I had gone to Boots for a box of condoms to keep in my bedside drawer. I couldn't remember the last time I had bought condoms, and it reminded me of that coming-of-age movie, Summer of '42, in which

15-year-old Hermie goes to a drug store to buy his first ever 'rubbers' but is so embarrassed to ask for them at the counter that he gets a strawberry ice cream instead. Absurdly, I felt a bit like Hermie. After all, whether you're a green youngster or a 60-year-old grandma, you don't want the shop assistant knowing your intimate business. Then it occurred to me that nowadays you can just pull stuff off the shelf and pay at a self-checkout till, where no one knows or cares what you're buying. So I bought my big box of condoms and, feeling pleased with my admirable prudence, installed it in my bedside drawer…although admittedly the box didn't get opened all that often.

After Franny and I have finished eating, as we linger over our Amarettos, I suggest that she too might like to try online dating, now she is single again. 'There's a whole world of men out there, Fran. A cornucopia. And not all of them weird!'

She shakes her head. 'Too dangerous. If my business rivals get wind of me being on a dating site they might try to trip me up somehow. It could cause all kinds of trouble. And can you imagine what Harry would say if he found out? Oh my god!'

'What do you care what Harry would say? You're free of him now, remember?'

We look at each other and she smiles. I think I see a flicker of uncertainty in her eyes, but it could just be the candlelight.

It was 10.30 when I got home that night, and after all the wine and the Amarettos, I was decidedly tipsy. Getting undressed for bed, I was down to my bra and knickers when

I had an idea. It was one of my impulsive tipsy ideas, obviously, but struck me as a good one at the time. I grabbed my mobile, stood before the full-length mirror on my bedroom wall, and took a snap. It was only mildly saucy, revealing no more than the typical lingerie poster in Marks and Spencer's, while being rather less suggestive. But it worked well, I thought. An effective lingerie shot. I texted it to the randy Ryan, who weeks earlier had asked me for a 'selfie' of this kind, with a short caption: 'Here you are.'

It took less than three minutes to get a return message. 'Holy shit. Why didn't you send me that before? I really want you now.'

'Ha ha! Get your Irish ass over here then.'

A little later came his rejoinder: 'Can you take a pic with the bra off and your boobs up close?'

Reader, I switched my phone off in disgust and went to bed.

$\mathcal{I}$t was another of my 'snap' decisions (get the pun?) a couple of days later, which led me to send my lingerie shot to Charles. I was sitting in the lounge area at my health club, shortly before aqua class, when I sent it. I'd grown bored of being all good and patient ('good' is a relative term here). A month had passed since our last tryst. He had promised to call and arrange to see me, but failed to follow through, always pleading that he was 'busy', and I hoped the photo might shake him into action. It did.

'Good to hear from you,' he texted. 'I hope you're well.'

'It would be great to go out for dinner and then come back to my place so that you can ravish me. I've been so looking forward to it, corny thing that I am.'

'Is that "corny" or do you mean horny?'

'Maybe both.'

To my delight he suggested we meet early the following evening at his favourite martini bar in the West End.

Me: 'Yes, maybe I should start drinking martinis. Will they have the same effect on me as Limoncello, do you think?'

'Even more so perhaps! Let's try it and see what happens.'

'I'm getting excited now. Glad I sent you my saucy photo.'

'I was going to call you anyway. But the photo was still nice.'

Charles met me outside the entrance to the martini bar, near Oxford Street. He was leaning against the wall and smoking a cigar, looking debonair. You couldn't imagine him using a chemical loo in some caravan crawling with spiders on the Norfolk coast, not in a million years. And I loved that about him.

After such a long gap, I put my arms around his neck and gave him a big, wholehearted smooch. But this appeared to embarrass him and as he took my arms and lowered them to my sides, he said in a gently disapproving tone, 'I don't think we should do this in the street.'

'Why? We're not in Dubai.'

We went down the stairs to the basement bar, which was cave-like and eerily lit. It had a vaguely iniquitous atmosphere, like some 19th century opium den. I liked it. Such a thrill after my usual West End haunts, John Lewis and Marks and Spencer.

It was early so the place was almost empty. We sat down at a table in a corner and Charles handed me the martini menu. It listed a dozen different varieties. Orange and cherry and vanilla and espresso and passion fruit and ginger and mango and chilli and the one that really caught my eye, chocolate.

'Wow,' I said. 'So many kinds to choose from. Which should I have?'

'Let's start at the top and work our way down.'

I could see Charles was in his element. He went up to the bar and gave the bartender our orders and watched with rapt attention as the young man did the measuring and mixing, shaking and stirring and whatever else he had to do – I had no idea, but it took a long time. Then Charles came back and set my drink before me. And I smiled up at him, cheerful and full of anticipation.

We worked our way through several different types of martini, although as I had suspected the chocolate was by far the best, in my opinion, so I had two of those. I felt pretty full after that but Charles suggested we go and have dinner somewhere.

As we emerged from the murky bar into the bright summer sunlight, I took Charles's hand, but as with my earlier kiss, this didn't go down too well. He let me hold it for a minute or two, then slipped it out of my grasp on the pretext of pointing to something down the street. Well, some people just don't like being demonstrative in public. Fine. I would desist.

We strolled around on St Christopher's Place and the narrow streets nearby, until we found a little Italian restaurant, one of those tight-squeeze eateries which serve traditional fare and always have at least one genuine Italian waiter, even in these ethnically jumbled times. Charles, tall and well-built Yank that he was, seemed an outsized diner at our small table in that small establishment, with Japs and Germans and other tourists edging past us down the narrow aisle. But this was the hub of London and it was humming and I was full of martinis and gazing at my date's handsome face and hearing his easy-going spiel, and everything was great.

Charles was explaining that red wine shouldn't be drunk at room temperature, it should be cooled down and it all sounded like rubbish to me but I didn't care. He asked the waiter for an ice bucket and plonked the bottle of red in it. If he wants it cool, I thought, we'll have it cool.

We ate our pasta and drank our cool red wine, and afterwards Charles ordered a couple of Limoncellos.

'Oh no,' I piped.

He looked at me in mock surprise. 'But you love the stuff.'

'Yeah but I've already drunk plenty and I'm mellow enough.' Then I added: 'As Woody Allen said in the unforgettable Annie Hall "if I get too mellow I ripen and then rot".'

He commented that he'd never much liked Woody Allen, didn't find him funny, and he had never heard of Annie Hall. This didn't surprise me. I had already discovered that I shared about as many common cultural threads with Charles as I did with Little Pup, only Pup at least had the excuse of having been born yesterday.

Charles ended up downing my little glassful of Limoncello as well as his own. Then we set off for his place. For the first time we would spend the night there instead of at my house.

It was a business-like flat, really half-home, half-office. The sitting room contained a mammoth desk with a serious-looking computer, and there were shelves stacked not with books but with ring binders. The modest kitchen area looked as if no one had ever cooked a meal there, it was spotless and there was little in the way of foodstuffs. There was however a large jar of olives on the counter. For martinis, I guessed.

We sat down on his neat two-seater sofa. I kicked my shoes off and, curling up beside him, gave him a tender kiss. Then I said: 'There's no one around now. So it's okay, right?'

He leaned back with his eyes closed and it wasn't long before I realised that he had drifted off to asleep. Well, it was late and he had put away a lot of booze.

But that, I knew, was just an excuse. In truth he seemed very much like a man who was unmoved by my charms. And as I scanned the unfamiliar and somehow unwelcoming surroundings, I felt my spirits droop. What could have changed between us in the weeks since our last meeting, which had held so much promise in its closeness and warmth? Or had I imagined it all? No, I couldn't have.

And what was with his allusions to my dating? A couple of times that evening, when my mobile tinkled to announce the arrival of a text or email, he remarked, casually: 'There's your next date.' I found this vaguely unsettling. It was as if he were willing me into the arms of other men. Did he intend to send the signal that he and I were just two people whose paths had crossed, randomly, on a dating site, that there was nothing more to it than that and I shouldn't view him as more than just one small part of my dating life? That I shouldn't read too much into 'us'? That ultimately he just didn't care enough?

Then again, perhaps he was only trying to protect me from disappointment and hurt. He had told me he planned to return to the States at some point, and that before then there would be a lot of travelling for work, lengthy spells abroad, maybe even a foreign posting. An emotional involvement would only complicate things and lead to a painful parting when the inevitable day came. Was he being tough with me in order to be kind? It hadn't been like that on our first two dates.

When we retired to his bed that night it was clear there would be nothing on the agenda but sleep. But there was always dawn's early light to look forward to, I told myself as I drifted off. We'll wake up rested and maybe he will finally be raring to go. I have my womanly wiles, after all…

But there were no morning frolics for us. Instead we lay in bed talking.

'Sorry about my lack of interest in sex,' he said. And then he uttered that most clichéd of explanations, which made me groan inside: 'It's not you, it's me.' When I turned to him wordlessly in a quest for more elucidation, he continued: 'I've got too much on my mind right now. I'm up to my neck in deadlines and all kinds of administrative paperwork.' He waited to see what response this would elicit and when I still said nothing he added: 'Men tend to go off sex when they're really busy with work and other things.'

'Is there anything I can do?' I asked, caressing his face.

'No. As I said, it's nothing to do with you. If I had Marilyn Monroe in my bed, offering me a blow job, I'd feel exactly the same.'

We got dressed and left the flat and he said he would walk me to the tube station, but along the way we passed a café with outdoor tables looking inviting in the morning sun, so Charles asked if I'd like to have something. We sat down and ordered cappuccinos.

We watched the world go by on Baker Street, silently for a while. At the table next to us a smartly dressed elderly lady was feeding morsels of croissant to the pug at her feet and for a while I gazed down at the little thing, mesmerised by its ugliness and greed. Then with a short laugh I turned away.

That's when, stirring his coffee, Charles told me what was *really* on his mind.

'I've spoken to my ex-wife a couple of times lately.' I looked up at him. 'We still have matters to sort out, administrative issues, joint bills to pay. Tedious stuff. Usually we do it by email but I thought I'd call instead. Guess I felt like hearing her voice.'

'And?' I took a sip of the hot cappuccino, hoping not to seem too interested. But of course I was all ears.

'I still have feelings for her. Not sexual, I don't mean that. But there's still emotion there. A kind of emotional dependency.' He peered down at the table.

'So...you haven't really moved on.'

'It was like I was betraying her, that last time I saw you.'

Now I studied the table too, not saying anything but feeling heavy and stupid. To think I had fantasised about introducing him to my sons and welcoming him into the family, and about his becoming the boyfriend, the *other half*. After only two dates! Stupid, stupid, stupid. And all the time he was holding a candle for his ex. Well I hoped it burned him, for making me feel a fool.

'I don't know if you can understand this,' he said, and our eyes met. 'I could probably have sex easily enough with the fat 26-year-old girl I once had that date with. Because that would just be sex and it wouldn't matter.' He paused, still holding my gaze, then carried on. 'But if there were something more involved, well...that's different. That's why I'm having trouble with you.'

I didn't know how to react. It was a compliment, wasn't it? But somehow that didn't help. My anger, on the other hand, started to dissolve.

'Could we see each other without the sex for a while?' he

asked. 'See how it goes?' He grinned and added, 'The sex was great, by the way.'

'You want us just to be friends.' I sighed. Friends. Like me and NiceMan. And *that* didn't exactly work out well. I was in danger of breaking another of Vanessa's sage rules: *never tell a man you can just be friends, they'll keep hoping for more.* Only this time the poor mug hoping for more would be me. I gave Charles a weak smile. 'I guess so. Okay.'

He gave me a brisk good-bye kiss outside the tube station and I gave him a wave.

I wasn't sure I knew what I wanted any more. But I sensed I couldn't count on Charles for anything, that there was nothing for me there, not now and not in the future. I heard his words about our 'friendship', but they struck me as hollow.

And the following day when I logged on to the dating site and saw that he was on it too, with the announcement that his profile had been updated and improved, with the addition of new photos, I turned away and shut him and his good looks and his urbane charms and his empty words out of my mind and out of my life. And it was all quick and clean, and at that moment I realised I was relieved that we were done. In the deathless words of that diva of divas, the inimitable Cher: *I've had time to think it through, and maybe I'm too good for you!*

As I had said to Francine, there was a cornucopia of men out there, waiting to be plucked out of cyberspace. Why hang about?

But I knew I would never look at a Limoncello the same way again.

CHAPTER THIRTEEN

We were splashing up a storm in evening aqua class and as Vanessa and I drew level she called out to me above the noise of the throbbing music and roiling water: 'I've had some more young ones contact me! I told them I'm not interested but have a friend who might be! They're very good-looking!'

'Great – send them my way!'

'Come back to my place later! We'll go online and you can check them out!'

So after we showered and dressed I drove Vanessa back to her flat, which I hadn't been to before. The place was memorable for the extensive wine rack in the kitchen (50 bottles, at least) garlanded with twinkly fairy lights. Nice touch.

She opened a bottle of *blanc*, got out a few dips and toasted some pitta bread, and we gossiped for a while over our girly feast before moving into the next room to log on to the dating site.

'Look, it's these two guys. Stud123 and Cruiser.'

They were in their early thirties. And cute. Stud123 was the cockier of the two, and his main photo showed him sporting a come-on smile, if ever I saw one. As it happened, both were currently online.

Vanessa quickly tapped out messages to them. 'My friend

on this site, called Raven, likes younger men and thinks you're cute. Why don't you get in touch with her?'

Before long I was messaging with the pair of them and they claimed to be in favour of pursuing matters with the game Raven.

'It's so nice of my friend Vanessa to give you to me,' I wrote to Stud123.

'Yes,' he replied, 'she's a good sport! And how can I be of assistance? Maybe pop round with a nice bottle of wine one evening to toast a new adventure?'

'Yes, that's the kind of service I like.'

'And I'm sure that other than opening and serving the drinks I can be of use in other departments...'

'I've no doubt that a resourceful young man such as you has many valuable uses. It would be nice to find out. So what is it about older women that appeals to you? The sophistication, wisdom, experience, self-confidence? Or have I missed something out?'

'The sex is far more adventurous, kinky and fun!'

My e-talk with Cruiser was more succinct. 'You like cute young men and I like refined older women, so we're both in luck. Would like to have a drink sometime if you fancy it.' And he gave me his mobile number.

I was chuffed that he regarded me as refined. Because it had seemed to me that in the space of a few short months of starring in my own personal Sex and the City show, I had gone from thoughtful fellow-journalist Carrie, my natural alter ego, to voracious man-eater Samantha. But that was all right, as long as I still came across as ladylike and refined... right up to the moment the knickers came off.

It had all got off to an encouraging start and I told the boys we would continue our encouraging communications very soon.

Vanessa and I chatted and sipped our spritzers late into the night, discussing men and sex and relationships. I asked her how many more good years she thought I could look forward to.

'Five,' she said without hesitation. 'You need to sort yourself out by the time you're 65.'

Her words were depressing. I had reckoned on, maybe, ten. The way that time was now hurtling ahead, five years would seem to flash by in five minutes.

Then she told me about her two girlfriends who had moved to Marbella years earlier, where they met and married rich English criminals on the run. 'They're having a great time out there with their bling and their swimming pools and year-round tans.'

'Maybe I should go out there and find myself a rich criminal,' I joked. 'I can get used to spending my days swimming and tanning and not worrying about money.'

Vanessa shook her head. 'My friends have both had boob jobs, they're thick, Barbie doll types. That's the kind those guys go for. You wouldn't stand a chance.'

Then she reminisced about growing up as the daughter of a publican and spending her evenings in the family pub, constantly surrounded by fawning men. 'In my twenties I would get a different guy proposing to me every week. A lot of them were rich and successful, they'd have been great catches. But after having my fun I'd tell them to push off. Easy come, easy go. *That's* what's given me the confidence that all these young guys like so much in older women.'

I had never had Vanessa's sort of confidence. I didn't grow up surrounded by fawning men and I had married the first person who proposed to me. Men didn't instinctively zoom in on me 'like moths around a flame'. Although I had always had my fans, I was something of a *speciality*, an idiosyncratic choice. But my confidence with men had been bounding ahead very nicely of late. And I knew I had online dating to thank for that. I was becoming sharper and more sassy. A bit of a minx, even. Good lord, I might never be the same again.

Easy come, easy go. That was what Vanessa had said. And in that spirit, Cruiser was the one who went – simply evaporated back into the ether, as these e-daters often did before any meeting could take place – but Stud123 came, all right. More than once.

We arranged for him to visit me after work one evening, and texted each other a few titillating messages the day before, to get into the mood (this was practically becoming standard internet dating protocol). This is an edited version of our message thread:

HIM: Can you wear something sexy?
ME: Like a frilly French maid's outfit?
HIM: Yes. Got a pic of you in one?
ME: No, but I have one of me in my underwear. Shall I send it?
HIM: Yes, I think you should.
ME (texting him the saucy shot I sent Ryan and Charles): Very
few people have seen this.

He responds by sending me a picture of himself stripped to the waist and flexing impressive biceps.

ME: Hmm. I think we'll get along just fine.

HIM: So do I. And if all goes well I can fit you in for a regular service when needed. Maybe we can even persuade Vanessa to join in. Lol.

ME: She doesn't do threesomes any more. Told me the last one was with her sister and some well-known footballer about 30 years ago.

HIM: Just us then. Maid costume at the ready!

We were in the midst of a rare London heatwave and Stud123 arrived hot and sticky. There was no preamble. We walked into the kitchen because I was going to get him a cold drink, but he jumped right into the proceedings, giving me a long, well-practised kiss whilst enthusiastically running sturdy hands over my backside.

'Did you miss me?' I asked when at last I came up for air. We laughed. He had warm brown eyes and an attractive smile. It wasn't long before we tumbled into bed. His speciality was raunchy, uninhibited sex – up, down, back and front, not forgetting sideways. An hour later it looked as though a herd of buffalo had stampeded across my bed. I looked pretty run over myself, as I lay in a sweat amidst the soggy, tangled duvet.

After a while I brought up a bottle of cold white wine and we sat in bed, chatting. He told me about his failed early marriage (he was only 21 when he'd got hitched), and about his family (grew up in Kent, divorced parents, didn't get on with the stepmum) and his job with a software company which didn't reward his talents so he was leaving to join another, where he would be more appreciated. He also spoke at length about the various areas of London he had lived in and their relative merits and demerits, although I was arguably more of an expert on London neighbourhoods than he was, considering I'd lived in the capital for 40-plus years and he had only moved there eight years earlier. But I know what men are like, so I listened patiently.

Then we had the well-established orgasm conversation. He said that he had always been very highly sexed ('You should have seen me in my early twenties!') but that he loved to give pleasure and the greatest satisfaction for him was the female orgasm. Such a prince! And I had deprived him of this great satisfaction.

I explained my difficulties and said the only thing that could do the trick was if I concentrated on sexy scenarios in my head, and I had a few old favourites to wheel out which worked well, but they were too dirty to tell anyone about. This was the first bit of information about me that really roused his interest.

'Tell me about them.'

'No, too embarrassing. They're secret.'

'Come on.' He stroked my hair. 'I won't tell a soul.'

'Nope.'

So he padded off to take a shower.

By now it was dinnertime and I had taken care to have some nice eats in the house: smoked salmon, salad, fresh baguette and butter. Ice cream for afters. After all the wild physical exertion, I was expecting my Stud to be ravenous.

But he declined the offer of a meal, saying he was trying to lose weight and being 'very good' about cutting down on his consumption. So although it was only 8.30 p.m., he bid me goodbye and headed off towards the tube station.

His departure left me feeling strangely deflated. It seemed as if, in some perverse way, we could instantly leap into the most thoroughgoing carnal pleasures with each other, no problem, yet somehow to sit down and have dinner together would be too intimate a thing for us for to do, seeing as we were virtual strangers. Dinner *à deux* was what proper couples did.

I went outside to the garden, sat down on the steps by the little fishpond and watched my goldfish and koi swimming in their meaningless circles. I was having a moment of existential angst.

Later I texted Vanessa, briefly filling her in on my 'date' with Stud, the younger man she had so considerately passed on to me. 'He came, we shagged, he left. Christ, what the hell am I doing?'

She replied: 'Are you okay, darling? Come over for a drink if you want.'

But I just wanted to change my bedclothes and hole up in bed with the comfort of my accoutrements around me – notebook and pen, radio remote control, mobile, mug of peppermint tea, et al. – so that I could feel like myself again.

Perhaps I was not so Samantha, after all.

I didn't think I would ever hear from Stud123 again, now that he'd had what he came for. But a text tinkled in late that night: 'I had fun, hope you did too. Would love to hear your dirty fantasies. Maybe next time?'

The following week it was back to The Bells for an initial drink with a new young friend, Simon. His dating profile caught my eye because it was so articulate, it contained big words and grown-up thoughts. I sent a message paying tribute to his superior language skills.

He replied: Thank you. Coming from a journalist, I won't take the compliment lightly. How are you finding online dating?

Me: Illuminating. Have discovered a fondness for handsome young men, and if they can spell and use proper grammar, all the better! [Shameless but such fun.]

Him: I hope I fit the remit.

Me: Oh I think you might.

Him: That's nice to hear from someone so alluring.

And we were away.

Simon was 25, slim, sweet-faced and boyish, a little shy, but one of those super-bright young men powering ahead on the cutting edge of the technological revolution. He was an internet entrepreneur and blatantly passionate about digital technology. A total geek, in other words, but in the most charming way. And with lovely manners.

We sat back in the squashy armchairs in The Bells (I thought the Sheena Easton lookalike barmaid smirked as she spotted me there with yet another young male companion, but maybe I imagined it) and he gave me his potted biography. Born and bred in salubrious Hampstead, intellectual parents, prep and public school education. When he mentioned that he still lived at home, I felt a wicked frisson shoot down my cradle-snatching spine.

Then, predictably, we got onto the subject of relationships.

'I've never had a serious girlfriend,' he admitted. 'It's so hard to meet people. Before the days of iPads, iPods, tablets and smartphones, people could strike up a conversation on the tube or in a bus queue. You could say to a girl, "Hey, you look nice, fancy a drink?" But now everyone is immersed in their own little universe. People don't even make eye contact. That's why we all use dating sites.'

He recounted a dating disaster with a girl he'd met online. She wanted to go to the cinema for their first date, and being a gentleman, he let her choose the film. 'Unfortunately she picked a really bleak Japanese film with subtitles. It was all about the dreadful lives of the members of a poor family living with the legacy of Hiroshima. A real downer. And very long. By the end of it we were both so depressed we could barely speak. We just trudged off in silence to the tube, said good-bye and never met again.'

'So the lesson is don't see a Japanese movie on a first date. I'll remember that.'

'Definitely not.' He grinned. 'James Bond, maybe.'

'How about blind dates? Do your friends ever fix you up with girls?'

'No, they're hopeless.'

I smiled at him. 'What would they say about you being out on a date with an older woman?'

'I don't tell them much about my private life…' He drank from his glass of beer.

'Would they be shocked and horrified?'

'On the contrary, it would be a big mark in my favour.'

'Even if the woman was my age?'

He nodded and grinned again.

Later that evening Simon came home with me. We had a cup of tea (tea before sex – so English) then went up to bed. As I had expected he was a shy, inexperienced lover, but all the more responsible for that – he insisted on condoms all the way, as per his sex education lessons at school, which weren't long ago. I love a sensible boy.

It was straightforward and pure, not wild and raunchy and all over the shop, as with Stud123. And at the end I rocked him slowly in my arms and ran my fingers through his hair, because I had warmed to him and his charming boyish ways, which contrasted neatly with his sophisticated mind. He was *refined*. I hoped to see him again.

Increasingly I felt that the big-bellied, baggage-laden oldsters on the dating site simply couldn't compete with these tempting young men. It was like looking into a cake-shop window and seeing all the scrumptious little cupcakes with their colourful swirly tops. Why on earth would you choose the boring old Victoria sponge?

Another young man, 29-year-old Harry, had been messaging me for weeks. I didn't know where he was from but his writing didn't impress me.

HARRY: How are you? You look pretty and have nice profile. I like to meet you and know more you. Let me know. I move to London recently and looking for love and fun.

ME: Thanks for your message but I might be a bit old for you. [Ha!]

HARRY: Age is not a barrier just it is a number. I am relatively attracted for relatively older women.

His looks were agreeable enough, and the reason I started ignoring his messages and hoping he would go away was not primarily because of his abuse of the English language. It was because, according to his profile, he was a mere five foot five inches tall. There were so many tantalising tall guys out there, why would I go out with a munchkin? I realised that I was being mean and that at five foot four I'm hardly an Amazon myself. Well, too bad. I saw it as a buyer's market and didn't want to waste my time. Life was too short. And so was he.

The old softie was becoming a bit of a bitch. But you can get away with that on the internet.

My old friend and fellow journo Andy Nott and I are having one of our infrequent catch-ups on the blower. He lives in Chester and I rarely go *oop* north, while Andy, a died-in-the-wool Mancunian, doesn't often venture to the soft underbelly of the south.

Andy, who is 58, was for many years the chief crime correspondent of the Manchester Evening News. His days were spent hanging out in sleazy dives with his bad-ass contacts – both coppers and crims – following up leads on high-octane news stories about gangland hits and drug busts. But these days he lives a sedate life of semi-retirement, tending his small garden.

Divorced several years ago, Andy has become more or less resigned to being single. He has said that at his age he shudders at the thought of going to singles' events, 'entering a room full of strangers and hoping to link up with one of them'. But now he tells me that a few months earlier his solicitous sister signed him up to a regional dating website. She had been urging him to do it for a long time but he always refused, so in the end she took matters into her own hands and the next thing he knew it was a done deal. For easy dating purposes, this site's members all lived within a reasonable radius of Andy's home. And it boasted hordes of northern lasses.

'So how's it working out? Meet anyone yet?' I ask.

He makes a sound like air escaping from a radiator. 'You've got no idea,' he says in a jaded tone. 'Every so often the site sends me an email with pictures of my latest "matches". These are women they reckon are most compatible with me, using some stupid computerised matching system they have.'

'And? Are none of the women any good?'

'*Good?* Listen, you know when I was crime correspondent I'd spend my time with murderers and psychopaths and gangsters who'd slit your throat in a heartbeat. But I swear to you, none of them were as scary as the women whose mugshots I see on that dating site. Some remind me of serial killers, and others, Jesus, others don't even look like women. They could easily be dodgy blokes in drag. It's all so depressing. And these are supposed to be the *compatible* ones. Who do they think I am? The Yorkshire Ripper?'

'Just keep at it, Andy. You need to be more proactive. Don't let a computer do the choosing, *you* do it. I'm sure there are some attractive ladies on there, too.'

'Yeah,' he says. 'Fat chance.' Then he makes that radiator sound again.

Every three weeks or so I had a visit from Pup. I always enjoyed seeing him. And by no means only because of our

140

amazing compatibility in bed, which in view of the age gap was little short of miraculous. I liked him a lot as a person and I think it was mutual. He had become a genuine friend, or so it seemed. I've no idea why he never inquired about my dating activities or even if I was still on the site, and neither did I ask him why he had de-activated his account (something I noticed one day whilst attempting to click on his profile) or whether he had met any nice girls lately. We never discussed any of those things, curiously enough. It was as if when we got together we inhabited a separate little world in which all those outside considerations were irrelevant. Or perhaps too awkward to bring up.

Sometimes I pondered whether, many years hence, when Pup was my age and I was, most probably, already registered on that misty dating site in the sky, he would recollect our times together – those dreamy days and nights he had spent in bed with a woman almost forty years his senior. Would he look back on them with affection? Would they remain his secret to the end of his life and make him smile to himself, in quiet moments when no one else was around?

Another thought which occasionally struck me and made *me* smile to myself, was that a year earlier, forlorn and despondent in the wake of the split from my partner, I had believed that if I were ever again to indulge in pleasures of the flesh with desirable young men, I would actually have to pay money for it. How naïve I had been.

Not, I hasten to add, that I was entirely unfamiliar with the act of paying for sex. Has that grabbed your attention? Allow me to explain.

A couple of decades earlier, during my single-mum period,

when I was sowing wild oats with gay abandon (attention: play on words) I had an urge to experiment in the Sapphic sphere. I revealed this secret ambition to a close friend of mine, much to his titillation, and he offered to buy me, as a birthday present, an hour with a classy call girl of his acquaintance. 'As long as you tell me all about it afterwards,' he said, 'so I can get the full vicarious thrill,' and I promised I would.

So my generous friend paid £250 for an hour of the blonde, buxom Penelope's time. And along with my first bicycle, at the age of seven, it was right up there in the top rank of my most memorable-ever birthday presents.

Penelope was kind and patient as she showed me the ropes. She showed me the handcuffs and face masks, too, but I declined them all. I was only interested in the standard girl-on-girl stuff.

Naturally I was self-conscious at first, feeling like a callow newcomer in the porn industry. But I soon entered into the spirit. Although I always suspected that Penelope faked her orgasm, as it seemed a little too pat and well-timed. I guess that's the problem with tarts. Sincerity. Not that I haven't faked the odd one myself, admittedly. But that was merely as a courtesy, not to encourage repeat custom.

I had one other Sapphic adventure, several weeks later. Another friend of mine, a long-time user of the services of prostitutes, told me about a friendly Soho brothel he frequented, which boasted a diverse selection of lovelies. I reckoned that as I had now sampled a Diana Dors type, it would be churlish of me to forego the delights of some dusky lady, too. So I booked an hour's slot with a diminutive girl of indeterminate Southeast Asian origin, with a thick mane of silky, dark hair.

She was pretty and smiley, as she carefully counted out the notes I gave her before pronouncing that I was, in truth, quite the most alluring creature she had had the pleasure of entertaining in many a long month.

We did the business, which was more relaxed now that I had been inducted into the fold and was no longer a total novice. That took the first thirty minutes. Then, in the second half of our playtime, the journalist kicked in. As we lay beside each other, chatting and fiddling ever more absent-mindedly with each other's hair and boobs, I asked about her work, which intrigued me.

She said she had a regular client who was a lesbian, a brawny, butch woman who 'fucked her just like a man, with a huge dildo'. Where's the fun in that? I wondered. Then my little lady of the night recounted an unusual episode with one of her male clients, an attractive married man in his thir-ties: 'One night he brought his wife along to watch. She was very pregnant, maybe seven, eight months, and as he fucked me she looked on and played with herself.' I found this story both shocking and oddly stimulating. It stayed with me and in time was added to my store of secret kinky scenarios, to be wheeled out as and when required.

And with that, my lesbian explorations came to a close. I always knew that that stuff wasn't for me. But the empirical research was ever so much fun.

CHAPTER FOURTEEN

$\mathcal{I}$ have never had an addictive personality. Never did drugs (not even in the sixties, when everyone I knew was high most of the time), could always go for weeks without alcohol if I chose to, managed to give up smoking without much bother, and gambling never appealed. But the dating thing...that was different. That, I could see, was becoming an addiction. And by dating, of course, I don't mean spending the evening in a wine bar, chewing the rag with some old codger, I mean getting intimate with seductive young men whose faces and physiques are pleasing to the eye. Once you've discovered that enchantment, how do you give it up?

Perhaps in vaguely similar circumstances Oscar Wilde had observed that 'where your life leads you, you must go'. Well, in the year 2013, this was where my life had led me. And whenever I was in danger of asking myself: what the hell am I doing? I would remind myself that I was my own greatest project and the project was coming along nicely, thank you.

Meeting desirable young men had proved to be surprisingly easy online. Then all at once it became a whole lot easier.

One day I was leafing through the paper and my attention was grabbed by an article about a new game in town,

144

an alternative to internet dating. Quick, simple – and free. Called Tinder, it was a mobile phone app which used its subscriber's Facebook profiles to access a few relevant details about them – first name, age, photos, location, interests – in order to match them with potentially compatible people within a specified geographical radius. You are provided with a flowing gallery of candidates, and on the basis of their photos, you can either pass on them with a 'no' or give them the thumbs up with a 'yes' – and all with a swift swipe of the screen. In other words, do you find them hot or not? When two subscribers mutually swipe 'yes' to each other they can open a conversation via the app and see where it leads. It all remains anonymous until such time as you both decide to take the contact further, moving on to other forms of communication and ultimately, perhaps, a get-together.

Ostensibly, Tinder was designed to help you meet new people for the purposes of 'dating, friendship or network-ing'. In reality it was a facilitator of casual sexual encounters amongst individuals who fancied each other…or thought they might. Its big advantage over internet dating sites was that no one could contact you unless you had indicated that you favoured them, and equally, if you fancied someone who didn't like you, they would never know, thus removing the embarrassment of rejection. It put you in control.

It sounded like a congenial arrangement. Why not give it a whirl?

I downloaded Tinder that evening, as I sprawled on my bed, the customary props around me, listening to Classic FM. Before long the app had taken what it needed off my Facebook page and my account was up and running. But when I looked at it I was horrified to see that it showed my actual age – a fortnight earlier I had turned sixty-one. It hadn't occurred to me that with this system I couldn't fudge my date of birth. Facebook knew *exactly* when I was born, even if that information wasn't visible to the public. Well that's a killer, I thought. No one will 'yes' a sexagenarian, sexy or not.

I really began to squirm when I realised, on surveying the stream of male faces presented for my delectation – each with their name and age attached – that these guys were almost all in their twenties, with some in their thirties and a very tiny number (desperate middle-aged specimens) older than that. But even the oldest I saw were a decade younger than me. It appeared as if I might be the most senior citizen, man or woman, on Tinder. A dubious claim to fame.

But I remained curious (and largely undaunted), so I proceeded to swipe 'yes' to some of the more appealing young Tinder candidates.

Over the next couple of hours, to my astonishment, I received a number of notifications from Tinder to say that I had been 'matched' with users who had seen me and given me a 'yes' in return. Bloody hell. You mean these twenty-something men didn't necessarily equate sixty-plus with decrepitude?

This had tremendous implications. It meant I would no longer have to fiddle the numbers (or as Pup would have said, the *noombers*). No more ducking and diving when asked how old my sons were, or being cagey about the ages of my grandchildren, at times even hiding their toys away behind closed doors so as to avoid the matter altogether. In short, in a curious way, the very anonymity of Tinder would allow me to be more myself. What a wonderful relief.

The Tinder door opened onto a whole new realm of young men, the really young ones, from the generation that didn't believe in paying for anything. Joining a dating site cost money and anyway, why struggle to compose a coherent profile narrative, why upload photos and list your favourite films, songs and books, and describe in detail your ideal date, when you can simply download an app to serve you up an instant smorgasbord of willing totties at no cost or effort to you?

Within a few days I had a small stable of fledgling studs ready and willing to play. Most were not long out of university. The youngest, at nineteen, was not long out of school.

This is an amalgamation of my various opening conversations with Tinder Boys:

TB: Hey. You look hot. Can't believe you're 61.

ME: Hello. Neither can I!

TB: So you like young guys?

ME: Yes, I do. Cute ones like you.

TB: Well, I love older women.

ME: Why is that?

TB: Always had a fantasy about them. They make me really horny.

ME: Would your friends be shocked?

TB: No. They know I get massively turned on by older women. I'm getting hard now just thinking about it.

ME: Have you been with older women before?

TB: No. I'd love you to show me how it's done.

ME: You're a very naughty boy.

TB: Yes I am...are you a naughty girl?

Pretty soon they would request a more revealing picture of me than the demure ones they had seen on Tinder, and I would send them my Marks and Spencer lingerie shot, which was always good for moving things along. And they in turn sent me DIY mobile-phone shots of themselves, sometimes showing rippling muscles down to the waist, but sometimes just a close-up of their erect penis. That always made me groan. Nothing looks more ridiculous than an outsize, disembodied dick. But you couldn't really take offence. They were only rascally boys showing off their wares. And anyway, sexual posturing was what Tinder was all about. And I was a kind of remote, electronic recipient for their raunchy fantasies, which I might, or might not, one day bring to fruition. But they had nothing to lose by all this bawdy badinage and exhibitionism. And neither had I.

A few of the boys got knocked out in the first round of messaging. There was, for instance, the one who preferred 'rough' sex. 'How rough?' I wanted to know. 'Plenty of biting and scratching,' came the answer. It sounded painful; less like sex than a fight between alley cats. Then there was the S&M aficionado who aimed to get all Fifty Shades of Grey on me, but as must be abundantly clear by now, I am far more M&S than S&M, so that was him dispatched back into cyberspace. (He was a lawyer, by the way, which somehow made sense…) But it was all huge fun, and wasn't that the point?

One of these young lovelies asked whether I was 'posh'.

'Rah-ther,' I answered.

'Brilliant! I love that! I'm imagining you to be a very posh housewife – very confident, very sexy and very kinky.'

'A housewife? Steady on!'

Which he countered with: 'Hey, this is my fantasy, not yours!' I had to chuckle.

It was the night of my first-ever Tinder tryst. Tom, a northern boy of twenty-one who had recently graduated from a redbrick university, was coming up from town, where he was doing an intern job at a financial institution, to meet me at my customary local rendezvous spot. He had already informed me that he couldn't stay long because his flatmate had locked himself out of their pad in Balham or Clapham or somewhere on the other side of London, so he would have to return before it got too late in order to let him in.

Kids, eh?

I was sitting on a barstool at The Bells when the tall, dark and dishy Tom, in a smart suit and tie, walked through the door. *Ding dong*. It struck me as apposite in more ways than one to quote the catchphrase of the dulcet-toned Leslie Phillips.

Tom was diffident at first – which I put down to his northern roots – but began to loosen up once he was holding a beer in his hand and we had eased ourselves down onto a leather settee to get to know each other. There wasn't more than six inches between us, but most women wouldn't mind losing their personal space to a bloke like Tom.

After forty-five minutes or so we decided not to order a second round at The Bells but have a drink back at my place. The problem of the locked-out flatmate became somewhat less urgent, as Tom texted him to say he should find something to do and stay out for a while – a nifty solution of my own devising.

I made Tom a sandwich back at my place because I know how hungry young men always are (in all senses of the word), but before he had finished it we started kissing and after a few highly satisfactory minutes of that, we moved upstairs to 'accelerate matters between us' as Charles might have put it.

Tom had had the same girlfriend throughout most of his time at university. She was a nice girl, he told me, but the relationship had run its course and was over now. He was ready to move on to more advanced studies. He had never been with an older woman but (as per usual) it had been a long-standing dream of his and if he hadn't been so northern he would doubtless have appeared more thrilled about the fact that it was finally coming true.

After the orthodox stuff I initiated him into the same practice I had taught Little Pup and for the first time Tom seemed genuinely excited. He loved this new game. Now his imagination was unbound. 'Hey wanna do a threesome sometime?' he murmured as he peered down at me, propped on an elbow, and smoothed back his damp hair.

I laughed. 'You planning to bring a mate along?'

'I meant with another girl.'

'I think I'd prefer to have your undivided attention.' Then I pulled his face close to mine and said 'Come here, my little cupcake,' before kissing his cute, grinning mouth.

Tom left at nine o'clock to take the tube down south, so as to let his hapless flatmate back into their pad. I, meanwhile, threw on my old dressing gown and flopped onto the sofa to watch The Borgias. I was thoroughly engrossed in the medieval mayhem when I got a Tinder message from another of my matches, 28-year-old Jon. According to the app he lived only a mile away. Initially, Jon was wary and insisted on verifying my identity. I gave him my surname so that he could check out my full Facebook profile and after that he was reassured.

'I'd like to come over,' he messaged. 'You up for that?'

'What, now? In the middle of The Borgias?'

'Oh, you'd rather watch TV. So disappointing.'

I thought about this for a moment. It was 10.30 and I was slouching around in my dressing gown, hair awry. Upstairs the bed was still a mess from my frolics with Tom and there were condom wrappers and tissues on the floor. But what the hell. This is the Raven we're talking about. And Jon's photos *were* captivating, which was why I had 'yessed' him. 'How soon can you be here?'

'Twenty minutes.'

'See you then.'

Ha – a booty call!

I whipped around and put everything into order, including myself – slinky dress, stylish sandals, tidied hair and fresh make-up.

When Jon emerged out of the darkness onto my front

steps, I was drawn to him right away. He looked raffish, with uncombed locks lying over the collar of a loose, casual shirt. He wasn't conventionally handsome (there was little about him that was conventional) but he had palpable appeal. I might even go so far as to call it magnetism.

As per the accepted procedure, we sat for a while as though at a job interview. He told me he worked for a recording company but his real passion was music and he was a part-time disc jockey. I told him about the louche DJ from Liverpool I'd had a relationship with in the nineties and he knew of him. Instant connection. We chatted easily, as though we had already been friends, and moved so naturally into intimacy it seemed almost preordained.

Where Tom had been an attractive, likeable boy who had entered our association in a commendable spirit of higher education, Jon was already a skilful lover whose every move and touch exuded finesse. He was a grown-up, unafraid to show real affection, and I felt almost drunk with pleasure. I loved everything that he did and every minute that we were entwined, looking into each other's eyes, rather too much. Because to my alarm I could feel it stirring long dormant emotions, and therein lay the prospect of pain. Sparking off that sort of fire with a Tinder match would be such a bad idea.

Jon left sometime after midnight and I went to sleep drained, sated, still flushed from all the love-making and thankfully too tired to think.

My next encounter was with Jake, a six foot three inch-tall, blond, rugby-playing 22-year-old, who lived with his family in South Kensington. He was so well-constructed that I would defy any red-blooded woman not to drool over the photo of him in swimming trunks served up on Tinder. Public school-educated and with courtly manners, he was not the type to send a picture of his penis. He didn't have to. I had already seen it in my dreams.

He came over late one evening after working out at the gym, as he did five times a week. I opened the door and there he stood in all his mouth-watering glory, like the statue of David. Only this David was warm and alive and as I was shortly to discover, far better endowed.

Jake, with his green eyes and open, friendly face, was so direct, so uncomplicated, he really brought home to me how much I valued these young men for their lack of neuroses. After this, how could I bear to face the wearisome hang-ups and emotional handicaps of middle-aged men? No, I mused, Jake and his kind might well spoil me for good.

We spent a fervent hour or so together and Jake, for all his impressive brawn, was gentle and considerate as we romped around in various enjoyable positions. Afterwards, as he put his shirt back on, he said he was glad I didn't turn out to be one of those kinky married women who gets guys over for sex so that her husband can watch. It had never happened to him but he'd heard about it and 'You can never tell,' he said with a wink.

'It was brave of you to come over, Jake.'

'And brave of you to let me.'

I perched on his lap as we waited in the kitchen for his cab to arrive. 'Do you realise there's a condom on the floor?' he said, pointing to a spot under the kitchen table.

I bent down to take a look and was mortified (although fortunately the condom appeared to be unused). 'God, how embarrassing! What must you think?'

Jake laughed. 'I don't think anything. Don't worry about it.'

'I have absolutely *no* idea how it got there. I assure you I haven't been doing *anything* in the kitchen.' Both statements were true. And ever after, wrack my brains as I might to figure out who had dropped the offending item under my kitchen table and when, I could never come up with any sort of answer. But it made me feel grubby.

Sara and I are in the sitting room with a bottle of red wine and an array of nibbles spread out on the coffee table between us. She's curled up in the armchair; I'm sitting cross-legged on the floor. I love our confidential girly catch-ups…even though I know what's coming. She has never heard of Tinder and I am explaining how it all works. And how it has been working for me personally, over the past week. It's only been one week and I have packed in so much Tinderness already!

'So you just give this guy your address,' says Sara, 'this enormous rugby-player who could squeeze the life out of you with two fingers, a guy you've never even *met*, and invite him over one night when there's no one else around.'

'Um, that's pretty much it,' I say with a sheepish grin.

'No one around to save you if he decides to attack.'

I dip a small piece of pitta bread into the houmous and munch on it. 'Nope.'

Sara shakes her head, hopelessly. 'What if he'd brought

half a dozen of his great hulking mates along to gang-bang you, before trashing the house and stealing your stuff?'

'Oh I knew he wouldn't do any of that.' I have to offer some rationale, so after a moment's consideration I say: 'He went to public school and lives with his parents in South Ken. You should hear him, he sounds like Colin Firth in Pride and Prejudice.'

Sara groans. 'You're a worry,' she says, before topping up her wine glass and taking a gulp.

'I'll be more cautious next time. Honest, I will.'

I was as good as my word. Heeding all the sensible warnings, I arranged to meet the next TB in a crowded public place, safe neutral territory. My address had remained top secret. Paradoxically, this assignation was with 27-year-old Benjamin, from whom the nation's womenfolk had little to fear. For a start he was only marginally taller than me and slight of build, not at all the physical type, and what with all my swimming-toned muscles, I could have easily grappled him to the ground in any rape attempt and sat on him until the cops arrived. But Benjamin wasn't the sort to rape anybody. He was an anxious Jewish 'creative' and part-time stand-up comic who did the rounds of the small comedy venues. The Woody Allen of Golders Green.

Not surprisingly, on first sight I was disappointed by the extreme contrast with my sex god, Jake. But I soon discovered over cocktails at a noisy West Hampstead bar that, slight and nervy though he was, Benjamin was entertaining company.

He had a day job as an advertising copywriter which he hated. 'Ugh. So stressful,' he said.

'What, and standing up in front of a room full of rowdy, boozed-up people and having to make them laugh isn't?'

'Actually I find it less nerve-wracking to deal with some nasty drunken heckler than with my bastard of a boss at work.'

I nodded thoughtfully. 'Yeah I hear you. I had some fearsome bosses at the Daily Mail, back in the day. Especially the Editor. I'd rather be pelted with rotten tomatoes and booed off every stage in town than have him tell me I'm a useless cunt.'

'So are you a useless cunt?'

'No!' I threw him a wounded look. 'I've been using it and it's worked every time.'

'Ha ha! Good to know.' And he raised his glass to me.

The longer we sat there talking the plainer it became that humour and intelligence can be as much of a turn-on as a great body and movie-star looks. And what with the bar crowd being so loud, making our repartee at times difficult to hear, I suggested that we continue the evening back at my place. Benjamin didn't put up a fight.

I sensed that he was less sure of himself grasping a woman in bed than a mike on the comedy club circuit. That, I presumed, was why he chose an older woman like me on Tinder. And also, perhaps, because the young women had been letting him down and he craved a change. He told me his girlfriend had left him two months earlier, a blow which had knocked his self-confidence. I asked whether he still missed her.

'I miss some things about her,' he said. And after a pause: 'She used to wake me up every morning with a blow job.'

'Bloody hell. That's beyond the call of duty.'

'A guy can get used to it.'

'I'll bet. Well, you won't get that sort of room service here.'

'Would you run to a cup of tea, then?'

'You got it.'

Benjamin stayed the night and we slept fitfully, stirring and fidgeting. He had told me he was a lousy sleeper, which fitted in with his Woody Allen-ish persona.

The next morning as I drove him to the train station he mentioned that he had a gig that night, at a small venue somewhere on the outskirts of London.

'Maybe I'll come along. I'd like to see you strut your stuff. I'll be the heckler at the back.'

We had a brief good-bye kiss and I said it would be nice to see him again sometime, on or off the stage.

Later I thought of texting him to 'break a leg' that night at his gig. But at his age, he might be unfamiliar with the theatrical saying and take it as a cruel and unwarranted jibe. You can never tell with young people. It's best to refrain from employing such old-school expressions.

I wondered whether our encounter – it was Benjamin's first with an older woman – would one day find its way into his comedy routine.

'So, what about these older women, cougars, they call them? You know, horny middle-aged women who've been around the block and really know how to give you a good time. I don't know about you guys out there but I've always had a fantasy about them. Oh yeah, the stuff of wet dreams. Anyway, one day I decide to give it a go and sign up on

Tinder. And there are all these hot young chicks of 22, 23, and I'm going "no, no, no", then I see my old primary school teacher and I go *"finally!"*...'

I just hoped I would be out there in the audience, laughing away.

CHAPTER FIFTEEN

Tinder was a playground, and as in any playground, there were some kids who didn't play nice. Zac, for instance, was a bumptious prick (I use that word for a reason) with scant respect for his elders and betters. Very early on in our messaging he told me he loved a 'really good long BJ'. It was the most important and most enjoyable part of sex for him and he always got what he wanted.

'I'm sure that as a cougar your experience will prevail in that,' he said. And he added that if I wasn't prepared to do it, as far as he was concerned it was a 'deal-breaker'.

I replied that, first of all, I didn't like being labelled a cougar. A cougar was a wild cat, a predator, whereas I believed only in relations between gladly consenting adults and had never preyed on anyone. And didn't cougars wear red lipstick and have long painted talons? Nothing at all like me. I was more of a pussycat, really. So much more simpatico.

As for his favourite practice, I told Zac it wasn't something I took lightly or did for everyone, 'only for someone I have feelings for'. I also tried to make him understand that going to bed with someone wasn't about being 'serviced'. A mature, experienced lover derived as much pleasure from giving as from receiving, maybe even more. *That* was real class.

'That's just a sucker in my opinion,' he retorted. 'Nothing classy about it. That's about desperation. Older men are so desperate for sex they'd do anything to get laid. Maybe you'd better stick to your older men, golden oldie.'

Golden oldie? Rude little shit.

Okay, let's take a moment here to consider the blow job. I don't wish to keep alluding to Sex in the City's Samantha Jones, but the woman had something cogent to say on pretty much every sex-related subject. I would refer you to her celebrated speech in Season three, Episode nine:

'You men have no idea what we're dealing with down there. Teeth placement, and jaw stress, and suction, and gag reflex, and all the while bobbing up and down, moaning and trying to breathe through our noses. Easy? Honey, they don't call it a job for nothing!'

Exactly. Unless you're a hooker, all this work is something you only do for a person you care about. And I didn't care for Zac, not one little bit.

Clearly this well-built, dark-haired 28-year-old, working for a bank in the City and living in smart Maida Vale, thought that any woman – and perhaps especially a more 'eager-to-please' older woman – ought to feel privileged to service his pulsating member. Admittedly it was an impressive specimen; he texted me a photo of it (oh yes, another day, another dick).

But I sent him one final message before deleting his Tinder profile: 'It's a shame we don't see eye to eye on these matters, Zac. Under the circumstances I think we'd better go our separate ways. Have a nice life! By the way, that's cougar for fuck off.'

The blow job figured high on the to-do list of another Tinder boy, the baby of the bunch, 19-year-old student Stevie. The idea of my engaging in rumpy-pumpy with a teenager was both alarming and titillating in equal measure. (Oh all right, it was more titillating than alarming.) This was not only because the gender-reversal age difference would be so monumental as to stand a good chance of making it into the Guinness Book of Records – he was forty-two years younger – but because I had never in my life had sex with a teenager. As mentioned earlier in this book, I was late entering the sex scene, having retained my virginity until the age of nineteen. And every man I slept with was older than me, not that I slept with many before marrying at twenty-two.

So Stevie could fill this gap for me, and by the sound of it he was keen to apply for the job. His photos showed a cute, slim boy with swept-back brown hair. He would do nicely.

He put his cards on the table at the start.

STEVIE: I've never had a blow job. Truth.

ME: Really? I thought you kids started all that stuff so early these days.

STEVIE: Not me. I'm a good boy.

ME: Are you really 19?

STEVIE: Yeah.

ME: They'll arrest me for cradle snatching.

STEVIE: I'll give you something to cradle! I like older women. I'm naughty like that.

ME: How old was the oldest woman you've been to bed with?

STEVIE: 56.

ME: And she didn't give you a BJ?

STEVIE: Nope. I just fucked her senseless.

ME: Well done.

STEVIE: Would you wine and dine me first?

ME: Hey, I'm not your sugar mommy. But I'll stand you a drink sometime.

STEVIE: Okay, and I'll treat you to a kiss. More if you promise to be gentle.

ME: Love your sense of humour, baby.

STEVIE: Can you keep up with me in the sac?

ME: I reckon so. And BTW, that's spelt sack.

It had all started so hopefully. But I'd forgotten how unreliable teenagers can be. They always have some excuse for not getting on with the tasks at hand. One of Stevie's excuses was that as an impecunious student he had little money for travelling expenses, and he lived an hour's train journey out of London.

We messaged each other now and then but never seemed to get any closer to doing the deed. I sent him the lingerie shot, to speed things up a bit. 'I can't wait to be inside that!' Stevie texted. But he did wait. And wait. Until finally I was compelled to give up on him. Honestly, you'd think I was asking him to tidy his room or mow the lawn.

Meanwhile Tom was keen to reconvene. In the days following our tryst (on that memorable Tinder double-whammy night) he texted me to announce that he was 'horny as hell' and asking whether he could come over. I said I was busy for a week or so but we could fix a date for after that. 'Can you behave until then?' I teased.

'Yes, I'm sure I can manage that. Can you?'

'No! Ha ha…'

'You had any sex since being with me?'

'Might have done. But I'd like to be with you again.'

'Shame we have to use a condom though.'

'We'll see, maybe not.'

'Got to be careful with you. You sleep around.'

I didn't like the sound of that. 'Sleep around? It's true you're not the only one I've been intimate with in recent times. But that's not what you'd want anyway, is it? Look, I enjoyed our time together so keep thinking of that until we see each other again. Be good, baby.'

'I don't know why you're telling me to be good when you aren't.'

His petulant tone annoyed me. 'Grow up, sweetie. I'm not your girlfriend.'

A week later I texted him to see whether he'd calmed down a bit. Actually, I rather fancied another roll in the hay with the comely young man. But when he replied it was to tell me that he was now 'sort of seeing someone', so things could get complicated.

'That's good, sweetie,' I replied. 'I hope she's nice to you. You're a lovely boy and deserve it. Get in touch with me again if there is ever anything I can do.'

'Thanks, that's nice of you. Still wanna fuck?'

'Ha ha…of course. But you're seeing someone!'

'I'm sure I can keep you a secret.'

'How very French!'

He then described in X-rated detail what he intended to do when he next saw me. 'Are you free tomorrow night? I'm supposed to be taking this girl out but I'll see if I can get out of it.'

'Oh, now I feel bad for her. Give her a chance and see how it goes.'

Crazy mixed-up kid. He was right, things had got a bit too complicated. Didn't need petulance or possessiveness. Those were for *relationships*. He couldn't handle me and I felt he was one Tinder boy who might be better off dating a girl of his own age.

We exchanged a few more messages at a later point, but he reverted to asking for sexy snapshots, as if he hadn't already seen all of me there was to see. 'Please, no more childish games,' I told him. And with that I put him into the box marked 'used Tinder matches'. In the Raven's opinion, there was no point prolonging anything that had stopped being fun.

Jon was the TB I most wanted to hear from, but he made no contact. With the tenderness of his touch he had reached something in me which was buried far below the surface and which I didn't even like to think about. It was a sentiment without a name, but had something to do, perhaps, with the need to feel cherished. And what a waste of time it was to moon over that! I had already stiffened my sinews against the likelihood of my never experiencing 'love' again, whatever that meant, if it meant anything at all. I'd had no lasting luck in that department, so it was safer to banish all soft, hopeful vulnerable emotions.

But the hour or so I had spent with Jon reminded me that

they were still there. I knew I hadn't imagined it. And although, obviously, the impromptu connection between us was nothing to do with actual love or cherishing, it was a compelling, irresistible facsimile.

I never did hear from him again. He didn't share my sentiments and I hadn't expected him to. Why should he? He had a future ahead of him, with its infinite promise and possibilities. For Jon, ours had merely been an enjoyable sexual encounter. Spontaneous fun. Tinder was awash with such opportunities for an engaging young man like him.

And if he had sensed, even faintly, what he had awakened in me, all the more reason for him to move on.

I moved on too, as things were kicking off with another TB. Damian's main photo showed a good-looking hunk with tattooed arms and caddish grin. He might as well have had 'fuck me, baby' stamped on those muscles, above the fire-breathing dragons or whatever they were. Damian, a power plant technician, struck me as an exciting sample of rough trade.

It all started encouragingly enough. On receiving my calling card, i.e. the by now well-travelled M & S lingerie shot, he messaged: 'When can I run my tongue down that body of yours?' A most acceptable opening gambit. Then: 'Have you always had a thing for young men?'

'Except for when I was young. Then I went for older men.'

He went on: 'Well I've got a real thing for women of your age.'

'Win win!'

'Yeah. It's rare to get an older woman into young men. I've been with a few but not often enough.'

'How old?'

'The oldest was 60 so you would take the honours. It turns me on knowing that you want my stamina and could handle what I've got to give. I get bored by young women who just lie there doing nothing. I like someone who can take the lead.'

I wasn't so sure I wanted to take the lead most of the time, but I didn't mention that. 'Sure I can lead if you like. Grrrr!!'

'I keep looking at your picture. You sure you're 61?'

'I think so.'

Then he revved it up a bit. 'What are you like down there, shaved or not? I like it not.'

'Uh-oh...'

'Ha, never mind! Can't wait to taste you.'

'Likewise.'

'And feel you up against my body.'

'I'm pretty keen to wrap myself around you too, sexy boy.'

Then his mental peregrinations strayed into top-shelf territory as he envisaged the specifics we might indulge in *à deux*.

Sara leapt back onto my shoulder at that moment, wearing her disapproving frown. I was doing it again!

'Wait a minute,' I messaged Damian. 'You've done due diligence on me [he'd been scrupulous, checking me out on Facebook, LinkedIn and Wikipedia] but I don't know much about you. Are you dangerous?'

'Very dangerous...but only if you want me to be.'

That was good enough for me. We set up a rendezvous for one evening later in the week. He worked about an hour's drive from London and we arranged for him to come straight to my place, natch, as it was so secluded and there would be nobody to rescue me should he turn out to be the energy industry's very own tattooed terror, scourge of womankind.

But I heard nothing more from him and when the day of our assignation arrived and I still had received no confirmation by lunchtime I thought I had better message him. It was early evening when he finally replied, saying he was still tied up at work. He would get back to me within an hour.

When he texted again it was to ask whether we could re-arrange for Saturday, a couple of days later. He still had work to do and wanted to get it out of the way. Naturally I smelled a rat. A super-horny guy like that wouldn't blow me out because of *work*.

'Can't you see me tonight? I'm all geared up for it. It's such a let-down to put it off.'

'I couldn't make it tonight anyway. The motorway's jammed because of an accident!' (Oh, so now it was a traffic problem.) 'But I'll make it up to you on Saturday, promise.'

I never even replied.

One day he's champing at the bit (or the butt) and the next he is all patience and the conscientious overtime worker, and I'm supposed to believe that? Call me a cynic, but I think I know men well enough by now to surmise that he had found some other piece of ass on which to lavish his attentions that night. Men, rascals? Let's not get started...

I'll say one thing, though. It startled me how blatantly shameless they could be. Witness Asian Tinder boy Rajesh. Tall and with striking, film-star looks. Naturally I 'liked' him and was chuffed when we were 'matched'. Then he sent a message, which said only 'DTF?'

'What's DTF?' I asked.

'Google it.'

I did, and it stood for 'down to fuck', a new slang term referring to those women who were game for casual sex. Ah, cutting to the chase. No niceties. 'Possibly,' I replied. 'But you'll need more finesse than that with someone like me.'

'Ha ha. Sorry. How are you today, madam?'

'That's better. So what about you? DTF?'

'Yeah. I'm in a relationship but always like exploring other options out there.'

The flagrant cheat! 'How would your girlfriend feel about you being on Tinder?'

Quick as a flash he came back with: 'How would your kids/grandkids feel about you being on Tinder?'

'They'd feel embarrassed. Not betrayed.'

Then he blocked me, even before I could block him.

I am on a girls' night in, Sauvignon Blanc and light supper in the kitchen. Emily is a few years younger than me, Carole a few years older. Both are friends from the enthralling world of London media folk. And both are single. But there the similarities end. Their approach to men and relationships couldn't be more disparate. And I sit between them, both at the kitchen table and in my viewpoints on those weighty issues.

Emily has never married or had children. She is a stead-fastly independent woman, beholden to no one. She likes it that way. For many years she has been involved with a married man and says theirs is a close, warm relationship and that the arrangement is mutually satisfying.

'We don't see each other often,' she admits. 'Maybe every five or six weeks. It's passionate and intense and about having a wonderful time together, rather than sharing every aspect of our lives. But that seems to be enough for both of us.'

'Good for you,' I say. 'And the wife doesn't know?'

'No and we intend to keep it that way. No one needs to get hurt. Actually, I think his relationship with me stops him from leaving his wife. It makes his marriage more bearable. I just hope she never finds out.'

I recall a famous Fleet Street journalist (and noted ladies' man) once telling me that his suspicious wife had the temerity to examine his emails and afterwards confront him with the evidence of his adultery. 'She read personal emails,' he declared in an outraged tone, 'with no respect for my privacy.' Only such an unashamed roué could argue that her betrayal of his right to privacy was a greater sin than his betrayal of their marriage vows.

'I had a few relationships with married men, a long time ago,' I say, 'and it was never a happy gig for me. Won't be going down that road again.' I mention that one married man, with whom I'd had a passionate affair 15 years earlier, wanted to stoke up the old fire now that I was single again. Our affair had started when he was newly married and ended six months later – abruptly and painfully – when his wife became pregnant with their first child. Sobered by the realisation that he was going to be a father, he no longer had the stomach for an extra-marital affair. But now that that baby had grown into an ornery teenager and fatherhood into a wearying role, a *liaison dangereuse* was on the table again. 'Looks like fidelity and commitment are fluid concepts for a lot of men. Most men, I'd say.'

'You see, I could *never* do that,' says Carole. 'I'd never have a relationship with a married man. Full stop. I've had a few invitations from married men but always point-blank refused. It's just wrong. And anyway, if I were in a relationship with a man I'd want it to be exclusive and not have to share him with some sad little wifey-poo sitting at home, pining away for hubby.'

Carole is the uncompromising sort. And generally believes that she is right about things. Her partner died nearly two decades ago and except for a couple of fleeting relationships, she has been on her own ever since. The problem, she admits, is that her standards are very high and no man she meets can equal her late ex. We discuss this impasse.

'You don't want to price yourself out of the market,' I remark.

'I understand about having standards, really I do,' says Emily. 'But it *is* possible to adjust one's standards without necessarily lowering them.'

Carole nods. 'Maybe, but it's not easy. And the longer I'm on my own the harder it gets. I'm used to having things the way I like them now, so I don't know if I'm capable of sharing my space full-time with someone else again. I don't even like having house guests for more than a weekend.'

'You've become too set in your ways,' I remark, feeling like the designated freewheeler amongst the three of us.

'Comes with age, hon,' replies Carole.

Emily asks: 'But you still want a man in your life, right?'

'Of course. Don't we all? Nobody wants to grow old alone.'

'So what are you doing about it?' I ask. 'Why don't you try online? You can meet thousands of blokes on those dating sites. There's got to be someone out there you'd like.' (I don't even mention Tinder; the notion of Carole signing up for that is surreal.)

'I'm too busy working. Haven't got time for all that futzing around on the computer. Anyway, the pool of older single men in London is a nightmare. When I tried the lonely hearts ads a couple of years ago every guy I met was either a ghastly bore or weird in some way. *Yeuch*!'

'And what about sex, Carole? Have you given up on it?' This is my specialist subject; I feel I must ask.

'Well, there's a problem with that.' She pauses. 'I'm wary about having sex with anyone because I always fall in love with the people I sleep with.'

Emily and I exchange glances. '*Always?*' asks Emily.

Carole nods. 'Yes.'

'Oh Jesus, Carole,' I say. 'That's crazy. You fought for women's lib back in the sixties, remember? I bet you burnt your bra. We'll never beat men at their own game if we can't control our emotions.'

She shrugs. 'Sorry, that's just the way I am. It's no big deal, though. Sex isn't that important to me any more.' She flashes me a pragmatic smile.

'Oh.' I smile back sweetly. 'I see.'

But I didn't really see. At this point in my life I didn't get 'throwing in the towel' with regard to sex at all.

CHAPTER SIXTEEN

There were another half-dozen or so Tinder boys with whom I entered into a dialogue which began with promise and heated up into a crescendo, only to burn itself out, usually for no discernible reason. But in a few cases I knew precisely what the reason was. Young people have learnt to be cautious in the virtual world and are mistrustful sometimes to the point of paranoia. There were TBs who remained unconvinced that I was who I claimed to be, suspecting that mine was a fake account and I was up to no good.

Admittedly it was highly unusual (probably unique) for a woman of my age to be on Tinder. So it seemed unlikely to them. There had to be something fishy about it. Was I part of a scam of some sort? One young man tried to 'catch me out' by inquiring whether I'd be interested in accessing his personal details, to see what my response would be. At first I hadn't a clue what he was on about. Later he friended me on Facebook to check my credentials and that set his mind at rest, although by then we had both decided that this was not a 'match' we wished to pursue. (He did inform me, though, by way of consolation, that his mate 'might be very interested'!)

And then there was Sam, who for me spelled the endgame. Our introductory e-conversation, late one night, turned quite ugly. Although he had 'liked' me on the app, which was why we were communicating, he soon began to doubt my identity, demanding to know what I *really* looked like. I sent him my popular little lingerie shot but he brushed it aside: 'That could be anybody!'

Then he became insulting about my age. 'Shouldn't you be making jam or something?' That was a bit below the belt.

I didn't know how to convince him I was genuine and was wondering why I should even try, when he sent me an obscene photo of a very fat woman doing something indelicate to herself with fruit. It was meant to shock me, like a slap in the face, but it was too stupid and juvenile for that, it just made me realise that it was past my bedtime and I should switch the mobile off. And switch Sam off, permanently. I deleted him from Tinder and my contacts list and went to sleep.

In the morning, without much deliberating, I went one step further and scrapped my own Tinder account. I had been on it for two weeks in total, encountered an intriguing little selection of young men and had had jolly good fun. A fascinating experiment. But the Sam episode left a sour taste in my mouth and I knew it was time to skedaddle from that particular playground. It had not been designed for the likes of me.

I was surprised, soon afterwards, to receive a text from Sam. 'Apologies if that actually was you last night. Had too many beers and got carried away!'

'Boys will be boys. Luckily I have a thick skin. [Not necessarily true.] Well, just off to make the jam now…or should I prune the roses instead?'

'Ha! Sometimes a thick skin is needed with me. I can be temperamental at times!'

'Is that what you call it?'

We had what seemed to be a pleasant exchange. I told him that, contrary to his impression, I was not a retired lady of leisure but a working journalist and directed him to my website. He browsed through it before messaging again: 'I'm shocked…you're a real person, who's lived a very interesting life!'

He told me he worked for a government department. Good lord, I thought, I can see why this country is in a permanent mess, with boozed-up government employees getting out of control, insulting the older generation and firing off offensive photos. Still, he seemed to have returned to his senses now.

'Sam, I'm glad we had that uncomfortable Tinder chat last night because it made me realise it isn't for me and I should get off. So I've deleted my account.'

'You probably made the right decision. There's a lot of testosterone flying around on Tinder, including my own. I suppose because you have no prior knowledge of anyone on there you don't feel guilty making outrageous statements. Well I don't!'

'I agree. Anyway, for me the whole thing had got a bit crazy.'

'I guess that's what comes of encouraging innocent young men. The lure of the older woman is overpowering!'

'Perhaps. But believe me, these innocent young men don't need much encouragement.'

'So…have I missed the boat? If only I'd been a few young men earlier.'

'Ah, I see. So now you're interested.'

'I was always interested. Just cautious.'

'Fair enough. Okay, I'm happy to meet, if you like, but will leave it up to you.'

Then came the final slap. 'Well here's the deal. You send me a picture of you with something relevant and I'm game. Otherwise it's a no go.'

'Don't know what you mean.'

'A picture of you today, maybe pointing at Tinder on your computer screen, something verifiable. Then there's no confusion.'

He was still confused? 'You're kidding. Think I would let some young guy demean me like that? Hey, meeting you isn't that important to me.'

'I don't intend to demean you. But it would be nice to put my mind at rest.'

'Then you can friend me on Facebook or connect with me on LinkedIn and we can send messages that way.'

'That doesn't help. Anyone can fabricate social media profiles. It's a picture or nothing.'

I might have replied, truthfully, that personally I did not know how to fabricate social media profiles. But I had wasted enough time on suspicious Sam and no longer cared what he did or did not believe. To me he was just an irritating greenhorn whose presence was no longer required.

'No deal.'

And with that, my days and nights of Tinder loving care came to an end.

*

At our last chinwag Sara had pointed out that some of those Tinder tots were actually closer in age to my grandsons than my sons. Only by a year or two, but even so, the thought was sobering (if only slightly). 'Try to date some men your own age,' she advised. 'You might click with someone. They won't all be like DanBoy and his dreary caravan.'

I mulled this over. I had loved being with young men. It wasn't just the robust, dexterous sex and the many pleasures of intimacy with delectable, strong young bodies. It was their company, too. Their easy banter, entertaining slang and youthful mannerisms. I loved it all.

But Sara was right. I ought to give the oldies another go. There were a few stipulations, however, which had to be met by any contender with whom I might enter into a liaison. Firstly, he couldn't have the same first name as my ex-partner. I had spent thirteen long years uttering that name and fancied a change. I was fairly open-minded about it but had a preference for short, zippy names. Drew and Clint, Tad and Tod, for example, were all perfectly acceptable. Secondly, he couldn't be yet another business consultant, like my ex. I no longer wanted to hear the buzz-phrase 'systems and processes' or the constant refrain of 'does that make sense?' at the end of every exposition. And finally, (yes, again like my ex) I'm afraid I couldn't countenance another fellow who took personal development courses and read self-help books. If I were to, as they say, 'get into bed' with someone (cue much chortling), I would insist that they already knew who they were and be content with it.

On the other hand, if the aspirant was hot-hot-hot, all the above objections would immediately be rendered null and void.

So, onwards and numerically upwards to the online old-sters. I decided to tweak my own dating profile narrative, making one or two minor concessions. Perhaps it had been putting some acceptable contestants off. Thus 'all men are rascals' became the more conciliatory 'most men are rascals'. And after 'I'm just looking to have a nice time' I added: 'but if something more promising turns up that would be a bonus!' (This was to encourage the serious prospects...not that I was anticipating any.)

I had grown strangely restless over the months of my internet dating. Once I had been reasonably content lying on the sofa watching TV of an evening or else reading in bed, and in the summer months, with their late hours of sunlight, taking leisurely walks in a nearby park. But now I felt an almost constant urge to be monitoring the doings on the dating site – checking to see who had, or had not, been viewing or winking or messaging me. Browsing through the never-ending parade of prospective matches. Checking the mobile for texts from my conquests (I use that word with irony) and if possible indulging in lengthy, risqué texting sessions, sometimes into the small hours, with any who were around.

It was as if I could never let things slow down, much less come to a standstill, I had to keep them moving, moving, moving. I always had to feel those wheels spinning under-neath me. And I wondered whether this was only a temporary character adjustment or had I been altered for good? Was this me, or was it the Raven?

I started to receive messages from a tall, grey-haired Aussie in his mid-fifties called Bob. An academic. Jovial but highly articulate (so refreshing), he displayed an agreeable touch of self-irony.

BOB: You are right. We men are indeed rascals, so nice that you appreciate us on our own terms. You understand us far too well, which removes any advantage of surprise. Not sure why you women put up with us…although I suppose we have our uses!

RAVEN: Yes, you have your occasional uses. Jump-starting car engines, checking tyre pressures…

BOB: And cuddling and other such delights.

RAVEN: Let's leave those for later, shall we?

BOB: Of course, women can be temperamental and irrational. While men are simply horny. But I will practise being charming.

RAVEN: Keep practising. You never know, it might work.

BOB: Less likely with someone who recognises men for our inherent shallowness and villainy! 'Tis all that testosterone washing about, an antidote to reasonable and rational decisions at times.

RAVEN: Ain't that the truth!

Once we had begun communicating on our mobiles, away from the sharp, supervisory eye of the site administrators, he seemed to go into libido overdrive, telling me how horny he was and that he would definitely have to 'cum' very soon. Hullo, I thought, here we go. *Et tu*, Bob? I had hoped for more. Then again, he was from Oz.

We set up a date. Bob lived in Chiswick and offered to drive over and pick me up to take me out for drinks and dinner somewhere nearby. A real, old-fashioned date. These old guys really did have their advantages. Cars, money, their own property, language skills. And the ability to drink and drive without hitting anything.

Bob turned up in one of the larger Mercedes models. Nice. I could get used to it. Must tell Vanessa.

It was a balmy evening so I proposed we have a drink in my tranquil back garden rather than at a crowded local bar. He readily agreed. I opened a bottle of chilled white, got out the olives, and we sat down at the garden table.

He was gregarious, in characteristic Aussie style, and enthused about my vine-covered pergola, the exotic palm tree, the row of towering bamboos along the rear fence and the fish pond. As we sipped the wine he regaled me with tales of his life and times. He was a fluent, intelligent talker and I was pleased that we agreed on the major political issues of the day, because life is so much easier when I am not com-pelled to leap into those predictable right vs. left battles in order to 'stand up and be counted'.

A divorcee, Bob and his ex-wife now communicated only through their respective PAs, and he did not often see his teenaged kids, who had moved abroad with their mother. But (unlike most Englishmen in his position, I imagine) he didn't seem too weighed down by these personal tribula-tions. And on the upside, as he pointed out, his present family arrangements left him free to follow his horny instincts on London's freewheeling dating scene.

He told me that one of the women he had met through the dating site and gone out with a few times later killed herself. 'Nothing to do with me. Apparently she'd been clinically depressed. Bit of a shock, though, to open the paper one day and read about her suicide.' Even the memory of this tragic incident failed to dampen his spirits, though. He simply popped another olive in his mouth and poured more wine.

He had also had dates with a couple of 'gold-diggers', attractive young foreign women (one Korean, one Nigerian) in search of a sugar daddy. Naturally he was shrewd enough to see through them early on, and his only regret was that he felt obliged to give them the heave-ho before managing to get his leg over. They were 'ravishingly sexy', he said.

Bob was likeable. How could you not like someone who can reel off the names of half-a-dozen eminent Hungarian scientists (and pronounce their names properly) while also telling you that you have a great ass? But I doubted there would be any hanky-panky between us, because I wasn't sufficiently attracted physically. I'd become spoilt. The seemingly inexhaustible supply of men online, including many splendid specimens, had made me highly pernickety. If a chap was too short, too old, too fat, too skinny, too hairy, too hairless, too big-nosed, too small-nosed, or he had bad teeth or piggy eyes or bandy legs…it was good-bye, Charley.

Bob had referred to the 'inherent shallowness' of men, but I realised I was being pretty shallow myself. Did the Raven care? No the Raven did not.

Bob had a fairly presentable appearance but his bulging belly put me off. After those firm, muscular Tinder tummies, I'm afraid that belly just leapt out at me in a way it probably wouldn't have done a few months earlier.

After the first bottle of wine he seemed in no hurry to

drive off to a restaurant, and as neither of us was starving, I opened more wine and brought out the dips 'n' crisps. We carried on talking as the light faded and darkness set in. Bob could expound engagingly on a variety of subjects and the hours rolled by. It began to look as if we would not be going out anywhere that night, and I just hoped that – despite his none-too-subtle allusions to matters orgasmic – he wasn't working himself up for a seduction attempt.

And isn't that the way of the world? While Charles, with whom I had been dying to go to bed, had gone all impotent, I knew full well that this wizard from Oz would have happily bounced away on top of me all night.

Every so often I went indoors for some reason and on one of my trips I checked my mobile and found a new message. With a delicious frisson I saw that it was from gorgeous sexy Jake.

Jake: Hey how are you? Up to much tonight?

Me: I'm on a 'date'! But would love to see you very soon. [And wasn't *that* the truth.]

Jake: Well if the 'date' doesn't go well you're welcome to come round to mine and we could have a nice night in. [Oh the agony! Tonight of all nights!]

Me: Sounds bliss. I'd love to have a romp with you again.

Jake: Come to mine later and you can have me anyway you want me. I'm in bed naked, wanting you here.

Me, attempting to eat my fist: Arghhh!

Jake: Enjoy the rest of your date.

I staggered back out to the garden, my equilibrium off by a few notches. When I got to the table, Bob's chair was empty. I looked around. He was sitting on the steps leading up to the pergola, doing something in the dark. As I approached I saw that he was barefoot and wringing out his socks.

'What happened?' I looked down at him, slightly alarmed. Even after numerous glasses of wine, the late hour and Jake's disorientating booty call, this struck me as a bizarre sight.

But Bob was as unruffled as before. He explained with a mild smile: 'Just having a stroll around the garden and forgot about the pond. I stepped right in, up to the knees. Hope the fish are all right.'

I put his socks in the dryer, thinking: that'll be another half-hour, then. No way will I make it to Jake's tonight. I sighed with resignation.

We moved into the sitting room and sat down on the sofa for more conversation. I glanced down at Bob's feet. As a rule I try not to look at people's bare feet because they are such unappealing things. (It beggars belief, to my mind, that there are actual foot fetishists in the world.) As I expected, his feet were really off-putting. Not the kind of feet I like to picture being intertwined with mine. Another reason not to go to bed with him.

It was getting on for 11 o'clock and I was tired. Bob was still lively, though, still full of stories and little asides (mainly sex-related), but well-behaved. To my relief, I realised that he was not the pouncing type. From time to time my mind darted to Jake and what I was missing, but the more tired I grew the less it seemed to matter. And still the socks tumbled on.

Bob left sometime after 1 a.m., giving my backside a playful squeeze in parting. He drove off in his Mercedes wearing his now-dry socks, carrying his soaked shoes in a plastic bag. He also borrowed one of my own books, thereby exhibiting a commendable interest in my writing career.

But it had not been the best night for the man from Down Under. He had missed out on dinner, fallen into a pond and failed to get any action, as it were, 'down under'.

But I hoped to see him again, if only as a social contact, because it's good to have raconteurs and clever people in one's life. But something told me he would not be content sticking to such a platonic role. As he might have put it, where's the cum in that?

I decided one day to send a conciliatory text to SuperA, my very first internet date. (Obviously I didn't count NiceMan, who still emailed occasionally to ask how my dating was going. But I thought it unwise to tell him about my capers. Why torment the poor man?) SuperA and I had been out of touch since our bust-up over his presence on the dating site on a day when he was supposedly hard at work. (To think I had actually been jealous. It seemed so ridiculous now.) A few months on, in my new, jealousy-free persona, I recalled that we'd had a good time together at our first – and so far only – meeting and I thought I'd try to reignite matters between us.

ME: Hello. Been thinking about you. You're not still cross with me are you? Why don't we give it another whirl?
SUPERA: Hey. Funnily enough, I did think of you the other day.
ME: Was it a nice thought?
SUPERA: Yes, I had a nice memory of waking up beside you with the sunlight streaming through your curtains onto your hair.

Blimey. He was waxing lyrical.

ME: Mm. And I have nice memories of you being on top and letting me have it with both barrels. Ha ha.

SUPERA: You were very irate with me, without reason. Why the change of heart?

ME: I wasn't all that cross.

SUPERA: You were beside yourself with rage!

Now he was overstating his case.

ME: I was just being a bit girly. I'm sorry. I'm so much wiser now in the ways of online dating!

SUPERA: Ah, I see.

Then he called me and we had a long chat. It was apparent that he too was in favour of giving us another go. He said he was very busy at work (of course) but would be in touch soon to arrange something.

I had meant it when I told him I was wiser. It had taken me a few months but I finally twigged how the virtual dating system worked, and why it was that dates and would-be dates would emerge out of the ether only to disappear mysteriously back into it. As the site members spent so much of their time online, there was a ceaseless ebb and flow of connections being created in varying degrees of looseness, and as new ones formed, earlier ones dissolved, whether consciously or unconsciously, it was never possible to know for certain. The hapless were dropped or forgotten or put on hold, whilst other options were explored.

Everything was built on shifting sand, nothing was solid or reliable or entirely real. A promise one day generally meant nothing the next. And the more you wanted to believe in the value of a particular connection, in its possibilities for the future and its potential for genuine emotion, the more likely it was to be merely a mirage.

In an environment such as this, there was no point in taking any individual or his words seriously, jealousy was negated and normal responses to other human beings – involving sentiments such as hope and trust – were deactivated. If you couldn't play this pitiless game, you were in the wrong place and had better get out before it hammered you into the ground.

My worry wasn't that it might hammer me. My worry was that I was learning to play it too well and might not know how to stop once I had returned to the real world, offline.

SuperA was appearing at a media event in town, had booked into a swanky hotel for the night, and invited me to go there and spend it with him. He wouldn't be able to get there before 11.30 p.m., but the plan was to meet in the lobby and he would then take me up to his room, which was on a high-up floor and looked out over the Thames. A late night tryst with a romantic air about it! I relished the idea of getting on the tube and gallivanting into town for hot sex at an hour when women of my age were more commonly tucked up in bed with cocoa and a copy of House and Home.

'Don't keep me waiting, though,' I told him. 'I don't want to hang about in the lobby like some Russian hooker.'

'Are you complaining already?'

At about 10 p.m. that evening I had just finished a languid soak in the bath and was applying copious amounts of body lotion to my limbs, when my mobile sprang to life with the merry chime of a text. I expected it to be from SuperA, and was startled to see that it was from Jock, the bearded Scot with whom I had spent the night in the Docklands, being hump-hump-humped into exhaustion. A blast from what now felt like the distant past in these dating chronicles. We had been out of touch for many weeks and I had assumed he and I were done.

'Fancy a shag?' Typically, Jock did not stand on ceremony.

'Yeah I do, actually, and luckily I'm about to have one.'

'Knock yourself out. You're a scream.' And he added one of those tiresome smiley faces.

You can wait a long time for an exchange like that. I smiled to myself and carried on with my toilette.

SuperA was only a few minutes late arriving at his hotel, looking smart in an Armani suit. I had forgotten how swish he was. He gave me a nonchalant peck on the cheek with his scratchy, short-cropped beard, as though we had only been apart a day or two and not a matter of months.

As promised, his room had a marvellous view of the skyline. But this was no time to be admiring views. It was late. So we got down to business on the deluxe, five-star bed.

It was all right but a bit mechanical, and for my part, an almost desultory affair. Not so much hot as lukewarm. Partly this was because I realised I no longer fancied him that much. I was fussier now. The slightly wonky teeth, those tufts of hair along his shoulders, the paunch I hadn't noticed first time around…these things stacked up and put me off. I couldn't just ignore them, much as I would have liked to.

But it was more than that. As before, SuperA didn't appear to have much interest in me beyond the sex. No curiosity about my life. I sensed once again that he didn't see the point in engaging me in that way, as our connection was only intended to be loose and non-committal. He was interested in one aspect of my life, though: my dating escapades. He inquired about them and when I recounted some of my more notable tales, he was all ears. He claimed to have been too busy working for any such shenanigans himself, and I felt maybe he got a vicarious thrill from my anecdotes.

Early in the morning, before there could be any chance of a replay, I got out of bed and got dressed.

'Leaving already?'

'Yeah, lots to do.'

We said our farewells but I paused for a moment by the door, turned back and called out, 'Don't be a stranger! Text me sometime.'

He was still lying under the duvet, expressionless, hands behind his head. 'I will.'

But he had undoubtedly picked up on my mood and I suspected he wouldn't be in touch again.

I felt light and free, walking down the empty hotel corridor to the lift. And on my way to the tube I stopped at a coffee shop for a takeaway cappuccino. Another day was beginning and as I strolled along the streets of the city I loved, the thought of it, for some mysterious reason, made me almost dizzily happy.

That evening, whilst lying on the sofa watching a cheesy

old western, I got a text from Charles. Just seeing his name on my phone again made me ridiculously excited.

The message was short: 'I'm thinking of you.'

My reply was even shorter: 'Me too.' I hadn't wanted to say that – shouldn't I play it cool? – but it burst out of me.

'Am going to the US tomorrow for a week but can we catch up after I return?'

'I'd love to!'

And despite myself, I let the hope creep back in.

CHAPTER SEVENTEEN

J'm lunching with my younger son at a restaurant near his office in Marylebone. It's a beautiful day and we occupy an outdoor table, enjoying the warming sun, and if it weren't for the po-faced Nigerian traffic warden sulking nearby, hoping to catch out some wretched motorist, we could be on holiday in a cheery Mediterranean town.

It is always a pleasure to spend time in my son's company. With his wry sense of humour, quick wit and tendency to shoot from the hip, he is great entertainment value. In fact that is also an accurate description of my older son, although the two brothers are strikingly dissimilar in other ways, namely their motivations and ambitions. The younger is in the world of international high finance; the elder is a social worker struggling to turn dysfunctional members of society into useful citizens. I adore both equally, it just means that when it comes to eating in West End restaurants, one is better placed to pick up the tab.

So we are having our light and healthy (if not cheap) meal in Marylebone and I'm sipping my refreshing spritzer, and not unexpectedly my son asks what I've been 'up to'. For a moment I ponder on what to divulge, what to leave out. Naturally I always give my offspring heavily edited versions of my dating life. I decide to relate the story of a date I went on the previous week, as it carries a U Certificate, 'suitable for all'.

'The guy had a terribly corny user-name which nearly put me off,' I say. In a mocking tone I tell him it is '*SpecialOneForYou*'.

My son rolls his eyes. 'Jesus.'

'I can't say his pictures set my heart aflutter. But he was passable. So in the end I thought I'd give him a chance and we arranged to have a drink in the 5th floor bar at Waterstones in Piccadilly. And when I saw him I was really taken aback. He was so much better-looking in real life.'

A tad warily: 'Yeah? How old?'

'Not much younger than me, he's 55.'

'Right,' my son takes a mouthful of food, relieved.

'We got on really well, talking about all sorts of things and laughing a lot. He was a very nice, bright, amusing guy. He said he was glad I didn't present myself on the site in a disingenuous way, like the last woman he'd met, who was pretty and youthful on her photos but in reality looked like a prune. At that point I admitted that, actually, I *was* a teeny bit disingenuous because I was older than it said on my profile, but he said he didn't mind, because at our age a few years more or less didn't matter.

'So anyway, drinks turned into dinner and we were there for three hours and there wasn't a single lull in the conversation. At the end he was a perfect gent, wouldn't let me pay for anything, and as we were saying good-bye out on the street – he was going in one direction and I in the other – I gave him a big kiss, then he said "next time maybe we'll go to a show" and I said I would love that. He said he'd call me soon. And I went home feeling very good about the whole thing.'

'The "but" coming up is deafening, Mum.'

I take a large swig of spritzer in preparation for the denouement. 'Well, two days later he leaves a message on my voicemail, saying that while he enjoyed meeting me and he'd had a lovely time, blah, blah, blah, he has decided he does not wish to "take things further". So he's saying, basically, good-bye and good luck.'

'Huh!' My son raises his eyebrows.

'Naturally I was stunned and disappointed. He was the first guy I'd liked in ages who was eminently suitable, or so I'd thought. Well, I didn't think I could just leave it at that. I had to know what it was that had changed his mind so abruptly, before we'd even been out again, before he'd given me a bloody *chance*. So I texted him to say it was such a shame, as I'd been hoping to see him again. And I said, maybe you can tell me where I went wrong, for future reference. And you know what he replied? He said, "You did nothing wrong, it's just that the *je ne sais quoi* wasn't there for me." *Je ne sais quoi*? Pretentious twat. Well, you know what? [I feel an abrupt surge of anger] He can just fuck off and take his *je ne sais quoi* with him!'

My son smiles. 'Oh dear. Someone's not taking rejection very well.'

'Listen, if he'd told me I was too old for him, or I shouldn't have smooched him on the first date, or he couldn't possibly go out with someone who wrote for the Daily Mail...well, perhaps I could understand. But *je ne sais quoi*? What's that supposed to mean? I don't know what that is.'

'Mum, that's *just* what that is.'

I pause and look at him. 'Oh, yeah. True.' We laugh.

'Mum, you're priceless.'

There is one other thing about SpecialOneForYou, which I do not mention to my son, but it is something that suggests I should be glad he decided not to *take things further*. During our dinner he told me about a woman he had met through the dating site and with whom he became seriously involved. They were together for a year. 'We had some wonderful times,' he said. 'She was a lovely person. Attractive, intelligent, fun.' He added, *sotto voce*: 'The sex was great.' I asked him what, in that case, had gone wrong and it turned out that what had gone 'wrong' was that the poor woman had committed the crime of falling in love with him. And it was not reciprocated. So he ended their relationship. Here was a woman with everything to offer, including the holy grail of the whole god-dammed dating business: lasting love. By the sound of it, she really had been the *special one for him*. But after leading her on a merry dance for a year he dumped her in the shit.

Je ne sais quoi? Oh no, I *do* know what. It's called being a bastard who can't commit.

I hadn't seen Pup in several weeks. First he had been away on holiday with his parents (so sweet!) and then he was studying hard for some professional exams he was taking. And if it wasn't that, then he was busy with his friends and his football. But at last we were in touch again and made a plan to meet. He was to come over on Saturday afternoon and stay until Sunday. Knowing we would be together again was a warming feeling.

On Friday evening I texted him to confirm the time of his arrival. As we exchanged a few racy messages in anticipation of our forthcoming shenanigans, I realised how much I had missed him and told him so. That was when, out of the blue, he revealed his secret.

'I have something to tell you.'

'How intriguing. What is it?'

'Um…I'm a cross-dresser. Sorry, I couldn't keep it in much longer.'

I stared at the words in the little yellow speech bubble on my mobile screen. Not possible. *My* Little Pup? My muscular, football-playing lover who was so indisputably, so confidently heterosexual in bed?

After five minutes of ruminating on this revelation, I texted back. 'What, you mean like you wear women's clothes and put on make-up?'

'Pretty much spot on.'

'I don't get it. I thought that was what gay or bisexual guys did. You're so great in bed!'

'Oh I'm 100% straight.'

'But then why do it?'

'I just like the feel of it and I guess it's my form of art. It's not really an issue between me and you.'

An art form? I considered this. Well, it was true that Grayson Perry was a cross-dresser and he was an artist. He was famous. No one seemed to mind him dressing up as a woman. Perry wasn't my cup of tea, a bit too freakish, and he didn't make a particularly fetching woman. Pup was bound to be prettier…But no, no, no. Where was I going with this? Pup was a *boy*. Not meant to be pretty. Meant to look like a boy. Besides, he wasn't an artist but an *accountant*, for God's sake.

After a few minutes, when he had received no reply, he texted again: 'Is it an issue?'

By now I knew the answer. 'I love being with you, Pup. You mean a lot to me. What you do at other times is your own affair.'

'You mean so much to me too! And I don't want to let you go.'

'Well I'm glad you trust me enough to confide in me. Not sure I really understand the whole thing but then maybe that isn't important. As Hamlet said, there are more things in heaven and earth, Horatio, than are dreamt of in your philosophy.' But as Pup had never heard of Neil Diamond, perhaps he didn't know who Hamlet was either.

'Thank you. My biggest flaw is a lack of trust. But your acceptance is a form of trust and I will be eternally grateful.'

The following morning he texted again to ask whether I still wanted to see him that day. Clearly he thought I might have had an overnight change of heart. But I said of course I wanted him to come, 'more than once'. Oh how I tittered.

It was true that I'd spent some time picturing Pup's boyish face fully made up, like a drag queen's, and those chunky thighs sheathed in some slinky, sequined number. And did he wear a wig? High heels and jewellery? It was all weird and somewhat discomfiting. But not for long. When he arrived at my door a few hours later and we hugged and everything felt just as it had before, I forgot all about the cross-dressing. It didn't enter my head again, not while we made love, not later on over dinner, as we chatted easily, the way we always did, and it grew dark outside. And not afterwards when, back in bed again as Saturday turned into Sunday, we enjoyed each other's bodies once more, doing things we hadn't got around to earlier in the day.

I don't know why Pup's revelation didn't disturb me unduly. Maybe because I'm a bit kinky myself. Or maybe I am just the consummate libertarian. *Leben und leben lassen* – that's me. But as I have stated here once already, nothing could make me think the less of him. He had said that my acceptance was a form of trust and I guess that summed it up. I just accepted. And I trusted that whatever he was doing was all right, really.

I was always a touch sad after Pup left to go home, and I never knew why, exactly. It obviously wasn't because I would have liked him to be with me all the time, a ludicrous notion. We inhabited different worlds in every way. The fact that every once in a while we could come together and meld our lives so joyously into one, however briefly, seemed to me nothing short of miraculous. Life is always teasing us with some enigma or other.

Perhaps the reason for the sadness was that each time I watched him stroll off towards the tube, I knew I was letting go, for weeks or maybe months, a little piece of unadulterated happiness. And those little pieces are so hard to find.

Charles's week away in America came and went, as did the following week, and the week after that. He didn't contact me for the promised catch-up. And so, once again I consigned him to the dating dustbin. But this time, I told myself, he would stay there. If he ever texted me again I would ignore it. Months earlier, when Charles first appeared on the scene, Vanessa had said she felt there was something 'dubious' about him. It seemed her instinct was right.

I noticed that, every two or three days, Charles went online on the dating site. You didn't have to be a stalker, the site flagged up everyone's status – whether logged on or not, how many days since they last 'surfaced' – and it was hard to miss. I wondered how the sexless-ness thing was working out for him, the self-imposed impotency caused by his hang-up about his ex-wife. Or had that been merely (so to speak) a cock and bull story? Presumably Charles was doing what everyone else was doing on the site: checking out the talent, winking and messaging and flirting and lining up their 'dates' like ducks in a row.

I understood what it was like, getting caught up in that. What I couldn't fathom was how anyone ever pulled the plug on all that swirling activity. How did you decide when you had met someone with whom you might wish to form an exclusive relationship and that it was time to turn away from all those other tempting prospects twinkling away in cyberspace? How did you ever reach the point of saying okay, I've seen enough, thank you, I've found this lovely person, we're a good match, now let's give it a chance and see where it goes? So long to all the rest, no matter how hot they are. And didn't that point have to be synchronised between both halves of the match? It wouldn't work if only one of you called it a day, while the other remained online and on the hunt.

To break the addiction a person might have to go into

rehab and attend months of supervised meetings. Date-aholics Anonymous. Or you could just go cold turkey, leave the site when the subscription ran out and return to the old system of trying to meet someone in a bar or at a social event or by bumping into them at the supermarket. A heart-sinking option, to be sure.

There was one upside to virtual dating, though, which hadn't been lost on me. It took the sting out of rejection. You were rejected so often – by those whom you contacted in hope, who in turn studiously ignored you, or by others who seemed genuinely keen before dropping you into oblivion – that it became something easy to shrug off. After all, didn't you do the same thing yourself to plenty of hapless contenders? And every lucky strike – the date that came off, the connection that produced something good and worthwhile, whether sexual or not, whether lasting or not – was a laugh in the face of those rejections.

I sometimes wondered what my ex-partner, with whom I had spent thirteen long and taxing, but faithful years – I'd been monogamous to a fault – would make of my current lifestyle. The romps with twenty-somethings, the dicey assignations, the unknown, untested men off the internet turning up late at night. The devil-may-care wantonness, the appetite for sex, sex, sex which at times seemed to be, in a word, Raven(ous). Naturally, I told him very little about my doings. And I reckoned that if he had known the direction my life had taken since our parting, the shock might have resulted in his spontaneous combustion. When he had last known me at close quarters I was fairly nonchalant about physical contact with him. As far as he was aware, I was 'past it', more interested in reading a book or cooking a meal, or anything really, than a roll in the hay.

And now here I was, a year on – at sixty-one! – and whilst he no doubt imagined me disporting myself with propriety, confining myself to fitting pursuits such as doting on my grandchildren and shopping for cushions in John Lewis, in reality I was femme fatale-ing my way around London. Oh baby, how fabulous was that? *Vivent les* dating sites, whatever their risks and frustrations.

At times I also recalled how, shortly after my partner's departure, alarmed by the prospect of an unfamiliar solitary existence, I had considered moving into an extended family set-up – an instant antidote to loneliness. What a mistake that would have been. It would have all but pre-empted my recharged sex life. Sneaking some man up the creaking stairs at midnight? Kiddies storming into grandma's bedroom at inopportune moments? Awkward introductions at the breakfast table? I don't think so! Sara and I laughed about this once and she agreed the arrangement would have been a disaster, before adding: 'Although at least I could have kept an eye on you.'

How long ago that seemed now. No doubt about it, I was wholeheartedly embracing the single life and squeezing every juicy drop out of my post-relationship independence. The debilitating hurt of those first few months after my break-up had by now dissolved without trace. I felt only the rewards of being unbound and in control. I was living a solo adventure punctuated by blasts of 'togetherness' with chosen others – blasts which at the best of times delivered pleasures and comforts, excitements and amusements. I was not beholden to anyone, I made no demands on anyone, I had no quarrel with anyone. In a peculiar way, despite my uninhibited and reckless adventures, I felt I was in a state of grace.

However, my graceful condition notwithstanding, I decided that after all the rumpy-pumpy it would be judicious to get tested for STDs, just to be on the safe side. So I went to a posh clinic on Harley Street and paid a lot of money to have them done lickety-split. It had suddenly become urgent for me to set my mind at rest.

I was relieved to get a clean bill of health, and showed it to Sara when we next met. 'You should frame it and hang it up on your bedroom wall,' she said.

I smirked. 'Like a diploma?'

'No, like a reminder to keep being careful!'

Vanessa and I were sitting in the steam room for a post-aqua powwow and she was describing her latest date, with a retired colonel. A widower. 'He took me to dinner at the Army and Navy Club, all very respectable. And he was a gentleman. Perfect manners. Really knew how to treat a lady.'

'Sounds like a success. Seeing him again, then?'

'Oh no. No way.'

'Why's that?'

'He was too normal for me. I like my men to be a bit off the wall. I'm not very good with normal.'

Of course, some men were *too* off the wall, even for Vanessa. A while back she'd told me about the man who took her home after a date and for some reason started talking about nappies. Baffled, she told him she hadn't thought about nappies since her son grew out of them two decades earlier, why the interest? And it turned out that he got his kicks from wearing a nappy in the run-up to sex and wanted her to put one on him when they were in bed together. 'I told him to get his arse out of my house,' she said, hooting with laughter.

Normal, off the wall. Hard to get the balance right.

Now there was another candidate in the frame. But once again he was too young for Vanessa, so she graciously offered him to me, as she had done with the raunchy Stud123, who'd turned my bed inside out with his exertions. 'You'll like him. He's just your type – early thirties, good-looking guy. Bit dark and Mediterranean, could be Spanish or Italian.' She cackles. 'You've got to read his messages. Very funny, the stuff he says in his wonky English.' She went all mock-lyrical: '"You are adorable lady, you are one for the kissing and cuddling, you my of cup tea, classy lady!" Ha-ha. Thinks he's Rudolf Valentino or something.'

It all sounded familiar. 'What's his name?'

She thought for a moment. 'Cosy and Fruity, something like that.'

'CosiFanTutte?'

'Yeah, that's it. Has he been on to you too, then?'

'Yep. Messaged me with the same exact words. *You my of cup tea, classy lady, you right up to my street.* Bastard. When did he message you?'

'Last night.'

'That's when he messaged me. Really makes me sick. This fucking game they play. I mean, if he had sent that bullshit to you a fortnight ago and got no joy, then came on to me, that would be one thing. But sending out identical messages to women – God knows how many of us – all at the same time. It's disgusting.'

'Oh get real. That's what everybody does. And we're not much different.'

I grunted. A case of Cosi Fan Tutte indeed. *So do they all*. I had got quite pumped up by the Italian's attention, which promised some exuberant Latin-lover frolics. Now it meant nothing. 'Maybe we're not all that different,' I said to Vanessa through the haze of swirling steam. 'But at least I don't use that scattergun method. And my English doesn't suck.'

Later in the changing room as we were getting dressed, Vanessa had a proposal for me. She was going out that evening to her favourite hangout, a smart bar-restaurant in Belgravia, to meet up with old friends. Why didn't I come along?

'I think you'll get on with them,' she said. 'These men really look after you. They're rich, never let you pay a bill.' She explained that she had been frequenting that place for many years and everyone knew her there. Her wealthy men friends plied her with champagne and she always had a splendid time, often returning home in the early hours 'completely off my face'. I asked what her friends did but she was vague on that point.

After months of meeting men online, the concept of being introduced to someone in the real world, perhaps even someone I clicked with, was strangely novel and stimulating. So I accepted the invitation. I suspected that a night on the town with champagne-swilling Vanessa and her moneyed mates would be fun, whatever transpired.

We both had our hair done that afternoon and got togged up in our finest. Then we ordered a cab and set off full sail for Belgravia. What a life. And to think Vanessa did this sort of thing all the time.

Her hangout was a sleek establishment with crisp white tablecloths and subtle lighting. Bold contemporary paintings adorned the walls and the bar was adorned by a handsome young bartender. I liked the place already. Parked outside it were a Bentley, a Porsche and something so high-gloss and rarefied in metallic blue I'd never even seen the like before.

Vanessa's pals were sitting at a large table by the window and at our entrance they greeted her enthusiastically. The bubbly was already in full flow. There were three men, in their sixties I reckoned, and a much younger woman, an attractive blonde in killer heels. They pulled up a couple of chairs for us and we were away.

They were an affable crowd and Vanessa had been absolutely right about the bill-paying. Whatever we wanted was ordered for us with a raised finger or nod to our waitress, a 'darling' here, a 'love' there, nothing was a problem.

Every once in a while I caught a flash of gold from a huge, elaborate wristwatch. The watches worn by those men looked as though they could fly you to the moon and let you play among the stars (sorry, Frank) and they weren't even Arabs. Judging by their accents and general demeanour, I guessed they were former East End boys made good. But *how* had they made good, exactly? I never did find out. I had a vague sense that perhaps I shouldn't inquire. There are times to be a nosy journalist and times to keep schtum.

One of the men, a silver-haired smoothie, was married. His wife was apparently at home, minding her own business, whilst hubby was out at his usual evening haunt, making jokey asides full of sexual innuendo. Another was a local businessman with an oily manner who seemed more hanger-on than Big Spender. I never noticed him raise a finger or nod for more of the booze which he swigged with gusto. The third was the one with the blonde arm-candy. He had the unmistakable appearance of a practised womaniser. She, on the other hand, turned out to be sharp and likeable, rather in the mould of those wisecracking Hollywood blondes, e.g. Carole Lombard. She had found her sugar daddy and I wished her well.

Vanessa and her gang gossiped about mutual friends, made in-jokes and regaled each other with anecdotes, often involving their recent globetrotting. They were friendly enough to me, if not overly curious as to how I had landed in their midst, and I found the scene absorbing in its way. But it wasn't *my* scene. And as the night wore on and we got steadily more sloshed (particularly Vanessa, who refused to eat any of the nibbles provided), I found myself hankering after my Tinder boys. A bit green maybe, impecunious probably, and certainly not in a position to make promises. But I would rather have been spending those hours with any one of my enticing, delectable and eager young men – although there was no future at all in it – than with that tableful of smooth-talking sugar daddies of mysterious provenance.

Maybe I wasn't yet ready for Belgravia.

CHAPTER EIGHTEEN

I had become used to the fact that the fanciable men on the dating site were almost invariably under thirty-five. The oldies – at least the ones who fancied me and made contact – were by and large a yawn-inducing bunch, dull in appearance and predictable in their statements. One older man, however, stuck out from the crowd. He was fifty-six but had eye-catching good looks – a youthful, smiling face, a full head of greying hair and blue eyes. He was evidently in good physical shape, judging by his photos, which showed him posing on skis as well as with tennis racket in hand. I expected him to ignore me when I winked, but a couple of days later, he winked back.

His name was Elliot and we opened a conversation, although it was intermittent because he only logged on to the site once every few days. I thoroughly approved of that. So many people seemed to squat there forever, indolently refusing to budge, like slugs in a vegetable garden. But obviously Elliot had better things to do.

He was a school teacher and sports coach and sounded breezy and direct. Divorced and with two grown children, he mentioned that he had been internet dating, on and off, for a few years. Had met a few women, but the right one hadn't come along yet. He declared himself an optimist, however.

When I showed his profile to Vanessa she shook her head and remarked: 'I would never go out with him. He's got those clean-cut, college looks.' She made it sound like a bad thing. But as I already knew, she didn't 'do normal'.

Personally, I was fine with normal if normal looked like Elliot.

It was true that he was a 'straight' sort of guy, given to following the proper procedures and protocols for online dating. Maybe school teachers had to be especially careful about that type of thing. Public sector political correctness and all that. So Elliot dropped no hints of sexy antics to come, there were no lustful undertones, nothing the slightest bit indecorous. After Bob the libidinous Aussie, he seemed positively eunuch-like. It was everyday pleasantries and politeness all the way. Obviously some, like Elliot, don't like it hot.

Finally came the satisfying day when we arranged our first date. Elliot lived in faraway Ruislip and suggested we could either meet in the West End or somewhere near me, if I didn't feel like trekking into town. How thoughtful.

I considered the options and one thing was for sure: I wouldn't be suggesting the bar at Waterstones. Never again would I have a potentially amorous assignation there. Following the flop with SpecialOneForYou (date venue: Waterstones bar) and back in the early days, my futile rendezvous there with Ramon, the sexless South American with the flowery spiel, I had begun to view the place as a dating black hole. So, with a comforting sense of familiarity, perhaps even inevitability, it was back to The Bells.

Tall, lean and tanned, Elliot came bounding in confidently,

looking like an American Vice President. He bought drinks and we proceeded, as per the rules of the game, to get acquainted. He was super-sporty and I wondered how much we would have in common, should we start dating. I didn't do sports. With every newspaper I read, the sports section was the first to be hurled aside, without so much as a how-do-you-do.

Indeed Elliot was so keen on sports of all kinds that he had been a volunteer at the 2012 Olympics just to be near all the action, and 'breathe in the excitement'. He described the unforgettable experience in detail, but I missed much of it because whilst he was nattering, I was speculating on whether or not I'd be shagging him later.

At one point he asked whether I had any hobbies and for a split second I was going to answer 'sex'. But I caught myself in time. It would have been meant as a carefree, spicy bit of banter, but I am sure he would have taken to his heels like a rabbit and I never would have seen him again. Elliot was not a spicy kind of guy.

At the end of the evening I offered to give him a lift back to the tube station and as it was raining he gladly accepted. During the short drive I toyed briefly with the idea of inviting him back for a nightcap or coffee. Surely, not such an outrageous proposal. Happens all the time in the movies. And he was certainly physically appealing, with all important boxes ticked: good teeth, nice hair, no beer belly, no scraggly beard. But I decided not to. He would have seen it as a come-on. Which it would have been. Obviously.

The truth was, I found it an easy decision to make. A few months earlier I would have tried it on. But not now. Despite his undoubted assets, I was fairly indifferent to the prospect of going to bed with Elliot. Perhaps we would do it one day, if we saw each other again. Or not, if this evening proved to be a one-off. It didn't matter to me greatly either way.

Was I losing my stomach for the mating game? I didn't think so. But something was happening to the Raven, that was clear. Could it be that she was beginning to feel a little too old for these larks? I thought about it.

Unlikely.

I'm at the pool, having a lie-down on one of the loungers after a long swim. It is late on a Saturday evening and there are few people around. My eyes are closed but I am made aware of someone sitting down on the lounger beside mine. Then I hear a voice: 'Hi.'

I turn my head lazily and open my eyes. It is a young man I have seen around the pool on many occasions, sometimes in the jacuzzi, sometimes in the sauna or steam room. Mid-twenties, medium height, medium build. Slight pudginess around the midriff. On the spectrum of male members at my health club – with tasty young dishes at one end, and fat, revolting slobs at the other – he is roughly in the middle. We have on occasion exchanged 'hellos' and smiles, but never yet spoken to each other.

'Hi,' I say.

He tells me his name is Brendan and he has been wanting to introduce himself. 'You really love your aqua, don't you?' he says. 'I've seen you doing the classes, really going for it. You're obviously very fit.' He peers at me with a serious expression.

I nod and smile at him nonchalantly, before turning away and closing my eyes again. Do I need this? I do not.

Brendan then tells me he is a lawyer, that he read law at Oxford, and is soon to be made a partner in a major firm. Furthermore, he has been writing a book about a crucial but little understood aspect of the law and it is going to be published soon.

I am not really interested. I wasn't that interested in the law during the seventeen years I was married to a lawyer, so why should I be interested now? But I feign interest, out of kindness. 'Oh, what aspect is that?'

'Can't really talk about it yet. It's a work in progress.'

Something tells me Brendan is not sitting next to me merely in order to discuss his high-flying career. I can see where this is going.

I do not have long to wait. A moment later: 'When are you and I going to go out for a drink?'

'Why should we do that? I see you here all the time anyway.'

'Ouch!' he says.

I give a short, low laugh to show that I bear no ill will. But I wish he would go away. For God's sake, this is my health club, my retreat. Not the dating site. Besides, I don't like the ungainly Crocs he wears on his feet. Although his bare feet might be even worse.

Next he blurts out, with no shame whatsoever: 'Would you consider a younger lover?'

I lie quietly but on the inside I'm groaning. I glance around. Luckily there is no one within earshot. 'Brendan, don't be silly. You seem a nice guy and we can be friends.

That's all. But thanks for the offer. I'll take it as a compliment.'

'No, no,' he says quickly. 'I'm asking for a different reason altogether. I have a girlfriend anyway, just to be clear. It's just that I've noticed an increase in the number of relationships in London between younger guys and older women. It's a distinctly modern cultural phenomenon. And I wondered what your view is on such relationships.'

I am greatly relieved. 'Oh sorry, why didn't you say so! Yes, I agree. As it happens, I am in a kind of relationship with a younger guy.' I am thinking of Pup.

'Hmm. That's interesting. May I ask how much younger he is?'

I am not sure he needs to know more than I have already told him. But this is a subject close to my heart, so he has finally piqued my interest. 'What have you been learning about this phenomenon, then? Do you have mates with older women lovers?'

'Well, I've had a few experiences with older women myself,' he answers. 'I much prefer the company of older women to younger ones. But generally speaking I'm not sure whether it's a fad or a function of a post-feminist society. In any event, there is something to be said for women having the right to equal sexual opportunities.'

'Amen to that!' Brendan sounds positively erudite on the topic and I am beginning to appreciate his company. 'In my view much of this particular dynamic has to do with young men not wanting to be pressured into commitment by girls their own age. Which is clearly not an issue with older women.'

'I think you're right. That's just one side of the coin, though. The other side is that there's a whole generation of older, divorced females who have decided that they prefer their independence to domestic bonds. As well as many women who never married at all and are keen to let their hair down. For women like that, younger guys represent freedom too.'

'Maybe you should be writing a thesis on this,' I suggest, 'instead of some obscure bit of the law.'

But he is still being serious and ignores my remark. 'I just think this is all psychologically revealing of the times we live in. It's almost a post-modern incarnation of a relationship. It's a relationship without a relationship. You know, sex and intimacy without commitment and responsibility. I think a feminist writer would argue, "well, if men can do it, why can't we?". But whether this really represents an advance for society, I'm not so sure.'

I am impressed by his lucid and insightful analysis. 'All very true. So tell me Brendan, is your girlfriend older than you or not?'

He turns away for an instant, as a middle-aged man with a towel wrapped around his waist passes us on his way to the jacuzzi. Then he says: 'I don't really have a girlfriend, as I'm sure a perceptive lady like you would have guessed. I was just trying to lull you into a false sense of security.'

I throw him a mock-stern look.

Undeterred, he continues: 'I was twenty-four when I had my first girlfriend. She was forty-nine.'

'Ah. Impressive.'

And a moment later: 'So, when are you and I going to have that drink?'

I close my eyes again and lie back very still on the lounger. 'Bye, Brendan.' And I don't move an inch until I hear his Crocs padding off in the direction of the men's changing room.

After our last exchange I thought I had heard the last of Jock the Hump, but he popped up one last time in one of his typically emoticon-enriched speech bubbles. 'Do you fancy hooking up again?'

ME (in jokey mood): Na, you're too old for me.

JOCK: I'm a lot younger than you.

ME: True, but you're a lot older than my toy boys, who are in their early twenties.

JOCK: Shame on you, baby snatcher. Your underwear is probably older than them.

ME: You're just jealous.

JOCK: Are you kidding? Well, it sounds like you're settled with your babies. Take care.

ME: If I took care I wouldn't have gone home with you!

Aussie Bob was not done yet, either. 'You realise that when we meet again I am going to try to seduce you,' read one of his texts. 'Fair warning!'

ME: Uh-oh.

BOB: I'll take you for a nice dinner first, of course.

ME: You said that last time. Then you fell into my pond.

BOB: That's easily done.

ME: Have you read my book yet?

BOB: Not yet but it's on my bedside table.

ME: I'm not impressed.

BOB: Don't worry. I'll bone up before I see you (no pun intended).

ME: Oh I'm sure a pun was intended.

BOB: Ha ha…Well, time for your water aerobics, isn't it? Got to keep that lovely ass trim. Don't ever want to see you at my monthly Porkers Anonymous meetings.

Not the man of my dreams, but it was hard not to like the guy.

The one whose appearance on my mobile I would have warmly welcomed was Pup. But although he always seemed genuinely pleased to hear from me whenever I made contact, he wasn't so good at initiating a conversation himself. And since revealing his big secret he had been even quieter. I wondered whether the two things were connected. Had he regretted his confession and was he now embarrassed and uncomfortable? I sensed him moving away from me and although I did my best to suppress it, I found it slightly upsetting. What of our friendship, our bond?

As the weeks passed I deliberately didn't message him, to see whether he would get in touch. He didn't. Had he met someone? The last time we were together he had assured me (totally unprompted) that were he to start seeing someone, he would let me know. Meeting a 'nice young girl' and going out with her would have been the natural course of events, only to be expected one day, and fine with me. Maybe that was it. And we all know how tough it is for males, whatever their age, to lay their emotional cards on the table. Easier to slip quietly away and hope no questions were asked. So I would not ask them. But it occurred to me that if he *had* acquired a girlfriend, she would be unlikely to have my *sangfroid* on finding out about his cross-dressing, which she was bound to do one day. She might scamper off in alarm.

Once or twice in a weak moment whilst alone, watching a film on TV or in the kitchen preparing a meal, I caught myself wishing Pup were there to share it with me. This, I knew, was a very bad thing. This I must guard against at all costs. Neither Pup nor Charles nor Jon nor anyone else who had got close enough to touch the core of me would be allowed to dwell for long in that vulnerable place where feelings are born and burnished and then buried. I wasn't the woman I used to be. I had become someone -- *something* – else. Raven. And while the Raven was not averse to a screw, she would let no one screw her over.

My next date was probably the strangest yet. I'll call him Nigel because that's a suitable name for a strange person. Don't get me wrong. Nigel wasn't scary-strange like MaxE8, the strangler; or exasperating-strange like Jabir, who was due to meet me at an Indian restaurant but was sipping tea instead at McDonald's across the road; or even hurtful-strange like *SpecialOneForYou*, who was indeed special, but not for me. No, Nigel was strange in a way that was totally his own and oddly disarming, and for a person like me who relishes human eccentricity, he made for an intriguing encounter.

Nigel was thirty-two and – let it never be said that I am a snob – he was a construction worker, the kind who digs up roads and then covers them up again, often for no discernible reason. Although he'd had a couple of long-term relationships, he had never been married or had children, and was temporarily living back at home with his parents, where he preferred to sleep on the floor instead of the sofa. He was no matinee idol but neither was he homely, and he was in pretty good shape – all that physical work paid off, obviously.

He told me he had been using the dating site for only three weeks; a woman friend had written his narrative because he 'wasn't much good at that type of thing'. I told him that maybe his friend should also have chosen better profile pictures to upload, as the ones he had on there were less than captivating, to put it mildly. The main shot showed him in hi-vis jacket and hard hat. Really! He admitted that I was the first woman to respond to a message from him, none of the others had given him the time of day, and I wasn't all that surprised.

Nigel had left school at sixteen with few qualifications. But although he was uneducated, he was by no means thick and he had a lot to say about the things which interested him, such as the cinema and television shows. He also gave me the inside track on the corruption at the heart of the industry in which he worked as a sub-contractor to various public authorities. I found that stuff quite illuminating.

It did amaze me when he told me – halfway through our drinks at the same trendy West Hampstead dive where I had met my little stand-up comic, Benjamin – that I was his very first date.

'You mean your first internet date?'

'No I mean my first date.' He took a sip of his rum-and-Coke.

I was baffled. '*Ever*? But you've been in relationships, so you must have been out on dates with those women. I mean, you didn't go straight from meeting them to living together, right?'

'No, but we never did this. *Dating*. Going out someplace for a drink or a meal.'

'Oh, okay. So I'm the first! How nice.' How weird.

He also admitted that despite his being English and working-class (a Londoner born and bred), he didn't drink beer or like football. In fact he had never watched an entire football match, he said, before making a grimace of disapproval to drive the point home.

Even more surprisingly, he didn't own a passport, as he had never travelled abroad and had no desire to do so. A curious proclivity for a Brit in the 21st century, the era of cheap foreign travel, multiculturalism and the EU.

As we strolled up the road to have dinner at a nearby Italian restaurant, Nigel looked around in wonder and confessed that he had never before been to West Hampstead. 'It's really decent around here, isn't it?'

Later, seated and perusing the menu, I asked him what type of wine he would like to have with his spaghetti bolognese.

He looked at me and shrugged. 'What do you think I should have?'

'A nice red. Chianti?'

'Okay! I've never had wine before so it's all the same to me.'

'Come on. *Never drunk wine*? I don't believe it.' I gazed at him. This was becoming surreal.

'My mum likes it. But I've never been interested.'

'Nigel, you're a one-off.'

'Do I seem strange to you?'

'Yes, you definitely do.'

'Other people have said that.'

'I'm sure they have.'

It was evident that this evening of firsts for him was making Nigel more than a little nervous, and he admitted as much. Throughout the evening he fidgeted with his clothes and his wallet and gave occasional nervous little laughs.

'Come on, Nigel,' I tried to reassure him. 'Relax. You needn't be nervous of me. I'm not too intimidating, am I?'

He gave another nervous laugh. 'No.'

In the end, though, he was too nervous to eat and left most of his spaghetti untouched. But he did fairly well on the vino front. 'Look at me, all posh!' he quipped as he downed another gulp of Chianti.

We chatted about Breaking Bad and The Wire and some of the films we were both passionate about, such as In the Heat of the Night, and it turned out that although he was half my age he loved Citizen Kane and The Third Man just as much as I did, and for the same reasons. So we did have some things in common, after all.

On parting, we agreed that perhaps we would go to the cinema together one day, and who knows, it might yet happen...

But it was unlikely. Because the bald truth of it is that those who have travelled all their lives tend not to go out with those who have never owned a passport.

As I said, Nigel was strange but not bad-strange. Just *very* strange. As I drove home I shook my head in wonder at a man who, for all his tough outdoor labour, had been living an extraordinarily sheltered life. It was hard enough to understand how a fellow could reach the age of thirty-two without having gone abroad or out on a date, or drunk a glass of wine or watched a footie match. But a man who had never, *ever* been to West Hampstead? How the hell did he manage to avoid that?

CHAPTER NINETEEN

The next time I met Vanessa she had important news to impart and wasted no time on idle chit-chat. In the bustling changing room, as we undressed for aqua class, she told me about Gerald, the new man in her life. They had spent the previous weekend together, the sex was fabulous, he had treated her to bucketfuls of champagne and lobster thermidor, ordered cabs for her right and left and generally treated her like a princess. As she packed her huge bosoms inside her bright pink swimsuit, Vanessa's face glowed with pleasure. 'He's taking me on a romantic break to Brussels next month, five-star hotel, the works.'

'How wonderful. Who is he? Not that last bloke on the site who said you look like Mae West and wanted to "come up and see you sometime"?'

She guffawed. 'No! We didn't meet through the site. Got introduced by a mutual friend.'

It turned out that she had met him at her high-class haunt in Belgravia one night when she was out on the lash. So after that long parade of online daters, hundreds and thousands of them over the years, and all the wink-winks and nudge-nudges and the computerised wizardry, she found her fella the old-fashioned way. Over a drink in a bar.

I knew Vanessa was after a stable, committed relationship,

so I asked whether she thought a fabled LTR might be in the offing.

'It's early days but the signs are good. And he really is perfect for me. Easy to talk to. And well-behaved.'

'Well, congratulations.' As we padded off towards the pool I asked: 'What about the dating site? Will you be coming off it now?'

'My subscription ends in a few weeks and I won't be renewing it. Gerald doesn't want me doing that any more. I have to respect that.'

She jumped into the pool and for a minute I stood at the water's edge, watching as she launched into a warm-up lap. I felt a stab of melancholy. She had been my internet dating companion-in-arms and co-conspirator. Now I would be going it alone.

I was pleased for Vanessa. But of course I knew this new relationship might not last. She might be back on the site again before long, giggling once more over the gallery of chancers and their predictable profiles, sharing with me the more fatuous of their messages over wine and dips at her kitchen table. It had been fun. And that fun had neutralised for me any discomfiture or tedium. Now what?

The immediate 'now what' was a date with a 36-year-old TV producer. We'd had a long phone conversation during which he told me he was up for some 'thrills 'n' spills' and I hoped his understanding of the phrase was more or less the same as mine.

Crispin lived in the East End and we met for a sundowner at a riverside wine bar near Tower Bridge. Judging by appearances alone, Crispin was not what I was looking for. On the short side, with slightly feminine features, hands a little too small and bottom a little too broad, voice not quite manly enough. Yes, I know I was being superficial and pernickety. But that's what months of ether-dating does to you.

Oh all right, the truth is I've always been like that. At the age of sixteen I went on a first date with a boy from my year at high school. A sweet-natured kid. He'd just got a brand new car and was keen to show it off, so he asked me out for a drive in it. It was a shiny red 1968 Ford Mustang fastback. Coolest set of wheels going. The boy wasn't bad-looking, either. Tall, fresh-faced, with wavy, sandy-coloured hair. It was a sunny summer's day. Car windows open, pop hits blaring on the radio, warm breeze blowing in my face. What could possibly be amiss? But after that ride I never wanted to see him again. And all because he was wearing a silly, frilly, see-through shirt which looked to me like a ladies' blouse and I couldn't take him seriously in it. I mean, I could see his nipples and chest hair through it. Gross! So I wouldn't even let him kiss me. Literally in the blink of an eye, he was yesterday's boy.

See what I mean? Utterly superficial and pernickety. In my time I've been hopelessly beguiled by some lying, cheating bastards. Love rats, scoundrels. No problem. But if you put the wrong shirt on, be you ever so saint-like, it's *hit the road, Jack*, Mustang or no Mustang.

Crispin told me about his TV job and his family and upbringing, and his past jobs and his travels around the world in between jobs, and his skills in Oriental cookery and his last failed relationship and why he now preferred older women (they were more stable and less exasperating). He was pleasant and well-mannered and smiled a lot and I didn't dislike him. And I smiled too and was pleasant back and was perfectly tolerant of his physical shortcomings. And in this spirit of tolerance and easygoingness, a couple of hours later I found myself at the small maisonette he shared with his two house-mates, being invited into a neat, cosy bedroom lit with red fairy lights, which gave it the feel of a dainty courtesan's boudoir.

He could, of course, have been a Jekyll and Hyde character, suddenly turning nasty and trussing me up with ropes. Or he could have been another sicko with a mummy fixation and penchant for strangulation. But fortunately for me, he interpreted 'thrills 'n' spills' to mean his continued niceness and doing everything I told him to do in bed, with a smile.

At the end of it I slowly got up and put my clothes back on. Resisting his entreaties to spend the night or at least stay on a while and have something to drink, I took off for home. He offered to walk me halfway to the tube station (this was his only failure of etiquette; he should have accompanied me all the way) and we carried on conversing agreeably whilst he took my arm and pointed out a few landmarks en route.

Although it had been a harmless exercise, I knew it was a mistake to sleep with Crispin, a man I didn't even fancy. But I had been borne along on a comfortable current of geniality, which had led me to his bed with a sort of passive inevitability. I had had sex out of politeness.

Really, I rebuked myself, I would have to stop being so blasé about the act of intercourse or it would lose all meaning.

*

A few evenings later I was waiting at a West End watering hole for Erik, who was Swedish. He was roughly the same age as Crispin, but a wholly different type. He had texted me to say he was running late so I had time to speculate on my latest date. His online profile presented him as a Scandinavian intellectual, a psychologist, no less. Clearly a man of substance, with a serious expression and dark, thoughtful-looking eyes behind a pair of thick-rimmed glasses. You wouldn't catch him sullying his messages with puerile emoticons and the loathsome lol. He was the sort with whom you could discuss the finer points of Nietzschean ethics, should you know anything about them. Which I didn't, obviously.

So there I sat, imagining what might happen when Erik walked through the door. He would be manly, smart and sexy, and all in a quiet, Nordic way. Strong but also warm. He would see me and smile and kiss my face on both sides, while giving my arm a gentle squeeze. And we would look into each other's eyes and just *know*. Something special was about to begin…

Naturally, when he arrived there was none of the above. What actually happened was that we had a 'shirt situation' again, as with that boy when I was sixteen. The first thing I noticed about Erik was that he wore a tailored shirt over his trousers which was clearly designed to be tucked in. Sartorial faux pas of the most elementary sort! But worse was to come. He smiled when he greeted me and in an instant that pleasingly serious expression was blighted by crooked teeth and I realised that he was one of those people who, for dental reasons, look much better with their mouth closed.

But there we were, in a bar, the evening was just beginning and there was drinking to be done, conversation to be had.

Erik, as I discovered, was an amiable bar-room companion. After the usual first-date chinwag we progressed to more brainy fare, such as his expert dissection of self-help gurus and their facile utterances, and his rubbishing of pseudo-psychologies like graphology and neuro-linguistic programming. I enjoyed listening to his analyses and we sniggered together at the quacks and crackpots.

If only he had been a friend or acquaintance, instead of an aspirant to milady's bedchamber. All would have been well and we could have met up again for more drinks and stimulating discussion. But I knew that wouldn't happen. As we strolled down Oxford Street on the way to the tube, he put his arm around my waist, for all the world as if we were already an 'item'. Premature actions of this sort are always a mistake.

A couple of days later he sent a text: 'So you didn't write to me after our date. I hope that doesn't mean you were kidnapped on the way home! Lol! Xxx.' And he ended with the most asinine of all emoticons, the one with the tongue sticking out. Oh Erik, how could you?

Next in line for the Raven experience was an Irishman called Sean. He was from Derry and sounded a bit like Gerry Adams but how could I hold that against him when he was thirty-one and hot and blatantly more into sex than politics. Just another stud with that by now familiar fantasy to fulfil. But Sean had specific requirements which he laid out, good-naturedly, from the start.

SEAN: Will you dress up for me?

RAVEN: As what?

SEAN: As a sexy older woman!

RAVEN: I didn't realise that required a costume change.

SEAN: I mean stockings and suspenders, high heels, lipstick, painted nails and sexy make-up. And what about lacy lingerie beneath your dressing gown?

RAVEN: I don't paint my nails and I hate lipstick (it would only get on your collar, ha ha). But I can do you some nice stockings and suspenders underneath my slinky little cocktail dress. Would that do?

SEAN: Def. Looking forward to having you sitting on my knee giving me a kiss. Are you going to talk dirty to me?

RAVEN: Um, how about 'show me what you got, big boy, me love you long time, hmm, you so hard'?

SEAN: Ha ha. Yeah let's start with that.

RAVEN: See you soon, my little Irish crumpet.

We had fun, Sean and I. He was thrilled with the discovery that I was sixty-one and a grandmother. 'That's such a turn-on!' he enthused. Men are a complete mystery.

This was the sum of our 'dirty talk' whilst doing the business:

SEAN: You're a naughty little granny, aren't you?

ME: Yes I am!

SEAN: Am I your favourite toy boy?

ME: Yes you are!

Not much, but it seemed to keep him happy.

Afterwards we talked for a long time in bed, with our glasses of wine, me still in stockings and suspenders, which felt rather silly after a while. He asked whether we could do a three-in-a-bed with one of my friends, as that was a supplementary fantasy of his.

I tried to dissuade him from pursuing this line. 'Listen, Sean, women friends of my age, whether or not they are grandmothers, aren't really like me.'

'None of them?'

I pondered for a while. 'Well, I do have one friend I think you would like. Jill. She's very pretty, blonde. She's divorced. And she's way ahead of me in the grandchildren stakes – she's up to five already!'

Sean perked up. 'Would Jill be up for it?'

'I doubt it. She wants a serious relationship, if anything. Don't think she does toy boys. And anyway, why would I want her to get in on our act when I'd rather have your undivided attention?'

'Oh don't worry, I would give you plenty of attention. But the thought of being in bed with the two of you – one blonde and one brunette – doing things to me at once, wow, that's so exciting.'

'Hmm. Dunno, I think Jill and I would just collapse into giggles.'

'Will you ask her?'

'Okay. I'll ask.'

After this I entertained him from my fund of sex-adventure anecdotes and he said he really appreciated being with a woman he found interesting and intelligent as well as attractive. I liked the way his words made me feel and asked him to stay the night. It would be lovely, I thought, to fall asleep together, all entwined.

But he wasn't keen on the idea, saying that it had only been a couple of months since he broke up with his girlfriend, it was all still a little raw, and spending the whole night with someone was a very 'intimate' thing to do. It would make him feel guilty so soon after the break-up.

I reckoned having sex with someone was fairly intimate too, but that obviously hadn't posed a problem.

In the end he fell asleep so heavily that he ended up staying the night anyway. He took over most of the bed and I nearly rolled off the edge twice. But he did clench his hand around mine several times, which I took to be a warm, *intimate* thing to do. Unless he did it without realising, of course, which was altogether possible.

I hoped we could have coffee together in the morning, and maybe talk some more. But he awoke very early, got up and put his clothes on without further ado. He bent down and gave me a kiss. 'I'll text you,' he said. Then he left.

He did text me, several hours later. 'It was lovely meeting you and I loved those stories you told me! Don't forget to ask Jill. It would be a lot of fun for me and for you too.'

'Okay, will speak to her tonight.'

When I called Jill and explained the proposition that Sean had placed on the table, she burst out laughing.

'Hey you've got nothing to lose,' I said. 'He's tall and has a great body, you should see his six-pack. He's cute, good in bed. Come on, it would be a riot!'

She finally stopped laughing. 'You'd seriously do it?'

'Oh why the hell not?' After a pause: 'I promise I won't

go down on you.' I giggled, to show her I wasn't taking any of it too seriously, and she giggled back.

'Well, it's not *my* kind of thing. And if that's really what he wants he might have to pay a professional to provide it.'

'I'm sure he wouldn't do that.'

'No, the younger generation don't want to pay for anything.'

Then Jill regaled me with her latest dating fiasco. She had been asked out to dinner by a wealthy, presentable middle-aged man she had met through her work as a publicist. He chose the restaurant – an expensive one – and ordered the wine, one of the pricier bottles on the menu. But at the end of the meal he studied the bill and told her exactly how much her half came to.

'The bastard,' Jill hissed down the phone. 'He drives a Ferrari but can't afford to pick up the tab for dinner? After he did all the choosing? It was more than I wanted to pay. So I just counted out the bills and flung them onto the table with a *harrumph*!'

'Bastard. I guess that's the end of that little relationship, then.'

Jill sighed. 'Oh I don't know, Maybe I'll give him one more chance.'

'Really?' And all I could think was: rather you than me, hon. Personally, I'd prefer to pull on my stockings for sexy Sean any day.

I am having lunch with my good friend and fellow journalist, James, in our favourite Soho haunt. The Gay Hussar is a famous old Hungarian restaurant – historic, even – dating back to the days when 'gay' simply meant merry. In the sixties and seventies it was always packed with lunching, boozing Fleet Street hacks, writers and politicos, gossiping and scheming and chewing over the issues of the day.

That was yesteryear. In modern times, as that old cast of movers and shakers has slowly left the stage, the place has become more touristy. But the food is still excellent and the decor is unchanged, its walls still lined with books and framed cartoons of public figures. So every once in a while James and I go there for a big blow-out meal – chilled cherry soup, stuffed cabbage, creamy paprika chicken with dumplings, chocolate and walnut *palacsinta,* the works. He is my senior by fourteen years and was part of that scintillating Gay Hussar scene decades ago, so he likes to relive his heady early days as a rising national newspaperman, when he gossiped with big-name editors, cabinet ministers and fiery trade union leaders over bowls of goulash soup and slabs of foie gras. I like to go there because the food reminds me of my mother's cooking and my Hungarian childhood. So we are both nostalgic within its aura, and contented.

James is, of course, aware of my internet dating escapades. From time to time I have given him little updates, especially as regards the more dodgy end of the spectrum, which makes for better copy. But this is the first time we discuss my dating activities in greater depth. James is particularly intrigued by the very young men with whom I've been having sexual congress (I love that expression for appearing to put sex on a par with weighty matters of state, which, for some of us, it is). The concept of the big age gap between sex partners intrigues James because he has intimate knowledge of it himself. He was sixty-nine when he became involved with a woman of twenty-one – a difference of forty-eight years. This is no mere gap, it's a chasm of Grand Canyon proportions. Remarkably, their relationship worked very successfully for five years and ended only when the lady in question left these shores to take up a job offer abroad.

James had often told me how 'sexually compatible' they were, that they shared the same sexual attitudes and 'tastes'. (The mind boggles.) She had bemoaned the inexperienced, enthusiastic but clumsy young men who did a 'rushed job' in bed, and could value James's mature, seasoned approach. As her father had abandoned the family when she was a small child and she had grown up without a father figure, he could fill that role for her too. He could advise and enlighten her. She loved asking him about things utterly remote from her own life and times, such as what it was like to live through the Second World War. And James liked explaining things to her. He had always enjoyed the company of lively, intelligent young people…as well as finding young bodies, young flesh, highly exciting. 'There's a reason why you don't get a lot of seventy-year-old pin-ups,' he once remarked.

Only his two or three closest friends knew of the relation-ship. 'Most other men would have regarded it as exploitative,' he says, looking back on the affair, 'or else just been plain jealous, as in: "you're exploiting that poor girl, wish I had the chance to do the same."'

'And what about her? Did she ever tell anyone about it?'

'No, nobody. Her friends and family wouldn't have under-stood what she was up to. If I wasn't her sugar daddy, then what was I to her? So the crude but obvious world view of the relationship would have been: what does he want beyond her body, and what does she want other than his money?'

He pauses briefly to refill our glasses with a fine Hungarian Cabernet, then continues: 'But reverse that and make it a relationship between a young man and much older woman, and it's even more bizarre and socially suspect. Society sees that as inherently ludicrous, like something in a Carry On film. There seems to be no biological or common sense reason for a good-looking, healthy and psychologically balanced young man to desire a sixty-year-old woman's body. I know it goes on, the cougar scene, but it's still a marginal activity and you think there must be something odd and unbalanced about those guys. I mean, look darling, I think you're fabulous and sexy, but then I'm seventy-five. So I was shocked when you told me about your involvements with these men of twenty-one, twenty-two and so on. Not shocked in a moralistic, judgemental way, but in the way I might be if you told me that, at sixty, you were going to start training to swim the Channel. I was worried about what you were getting into. That you might be inviting danger of some kind, either physical or psychological.'

I am somewhat miffed at the suggestion that a young guy has to be unbalanced in order to enjoy being my sexual congressman. 'One or two were a bit odd,' I say, thinking mainly of Max. 'And several were vulgar and juvenile. But I can vouch for most of them being pretty sound of mind, as well as body. They just prefer a woman who's experienced and mature and confident. In the same way as your young lover chose you over the rookies with their "rushed jobs", even though I suspect they had better physiques.'

He smiles. 'Hmm. Touché.'

But a little later, as we dig into our Magyar puddings, washed down with glasses of sweet Tokay, he airs a further note of warning. 'We're both of us off-centre in our attitudes to sex, emotions and relationships, while the rest of the world, by and large, is still pretty conventional. But people will be more disapproving of you than of me. They'll look at some elderly chap with a young girl on his arm and think, you dirty old man. Still, it isn't that unusual a sight and no one gets too wound up about it. But society doesn't much like cougar liaisons, they're too outlandish, too hard to fathom. And however liberal and progressive we become, I'm afraid I don't think that will ever change.'

I muse on this. 'Well, I guess I'll just have to not care what society thinks. After all, it's not like I'm drowning kittens. Us old girls just wanna have fun.'

'I'll drink to that,' says James. We clink our glasses, then talk of other things.

CHAPTER TWENTY

I was restless late one night, as I lay in bed amongst my standard props. The spring and summer of my dating chronicles had come and gone, we were well into the chilly darkness of mid-autumn evenings, and I had a hot-water bottle under my feet. I reflected on my past six months and what I had to show for it. There had been some high points, for sure, which I would not have missed for anything. Moments during which I had felt exhilaratingly alive, akin to other moments from my steadily receding past, such as when I rode pillion my on ex's motorbike and we roared through the glorious backdrops of France and Italy, glimpsing vineyards and olive groves and hilltop castles as we hurtled past.

Just as I had always sensed that my wild days as a biker chick couldn't last forever, I now felt my internet dating exploits edging towards some sort of culmination. I couldn't yet see how things would play out. But they couldn't go on like this for much longer, that much I knew in my bones.

I hadn't expected to find love, I hadn't been searching for it, I wasn't even sure I wanted it. Like fairies and unicorns, 'true love' was meant for children's storybooks. So, what I was feeling that night as I fiddled with my mobile phone to the gentle strains of Chopin emanating from the radio, wasn't disappointment. It was a vague dissatisfaction, a dull aching in some part of me because something was not right.

I had kept dozens of message threads on my mobile, long exchanges with dating matches and Tinder boys, both those I had met and got to know (biblically or not) and those with whom I'd merely had electronic 'relationships', who existed, as far as I was concerned, only in yellow speech bubbles on a Samsung. Few people seemed to want to talk on the phone any more, to let you hear their voices, as though that was giving too much away, too soon. They made all kinds of excuses not to. Which meant that I had this visual record of messages from my year of dating dangerously, my *grand projet*. Yes, I had been my own project and it had indeed been grand, in many ways. I had showed myself that, like the supreme Cher, I believed in life after love. Great succulent dollops of life. And I didn't care who knew it. But you have to bring every project to an end at some point, however reluctantly.

Now I was scrolling down the speech bubbles, reliving the emotional jolts and jitters, the thwarted expectations and the semi-gratifications of those messages and the self-contained little tales they told. Naturally I had deleted already all the prick pics dispatched to me, unbidden, by the hyper-horny brigade. The most recent had come from a forty-three-year-old who should have known better. I was nearly sick when I viewed his portrait of a slimy-looking penis and wrinkled testicles. At the same time he asked me to take a photo of myself 'being wet'. Oh yes, of course, that's what people like me do *all the time*, that's exactly what published authors and Fleet Street feature writers and grandmothers in their seventh decade who shop at Waitrose do *with alacrity*, you have only to ask. When I told this middle-aged asshole he was puerile and disgusting, he replied simply 'bye then', like a stroppy teenager. Easy to see why he was still single.

It was astonishing how often my derrière figured in those text conversations. I hadn't realised before how obsessed men – especially young men – are with arses, every which way. So for any ladies out there wishing to shed surplus fat in that area in order to acquire the more streamlined bottom which sends the opposite sex into paroxysms of delight, the solution is very simple, really. Go swimming for an hour five times a week and never give a Big Mac or Krispy Kreme donut so much as a passing thought. See? Easy!

I ran through the stream of messages I had exchanged with Charles. I never replied to his last one, in which he apologised for being out of touch for six weeks and repeated, yet again, that old chestnut of 'it's not you, it's me' (could he not learn some other clichés?). He said he was spending '100% of his time' working and had cut his social life 'back to zero', but I didn't bat an eyelid when I saw, the very next day, that he was active on the dating site. Not quite 100% of his time, then.

I stopped trying to figure him out, this man I had fool-ishly once felt might turn out to be 'the one', even though I hadn't been in quest of a serious partner. I had no idea what his issue was, and doubted I ever would. Was it really to do with his wife and an inability to move on? Or was he plagued by a Hamlet-like indecision, an inertia in matters of the heart, a fear of 'entanglement'? But if that was the case, why send me periodic messages saying he hoped to see me again at some future point? Why not just drop me completely? Didn't know. Didn't care. Give him his due, though. He could write a complete sentence without a spelling mistake, a lol or a smiley face.

Then there was Pup, with whom I had recently tried to get a dialogue going, hoping to tempt him over to see me. He, too, apologised and claimed to be 'very busy lately, all work and no play'. He didn't suggest getting together and as I couldn't *feel the love* beaming towards me through the ether, neither did I. I had been more emotionally intimate with him than anyone else throughout my dating annals. But he made it clear enough, without saying so, that he could get by without the Raven's attentions. So perhaps the time had come to say good-bye. I wanted to send him one last text: 'Bow-wow, Little Pup! Remember me? I'm the mature older woman who taught you how to go up the butt, who was so understanding about your kinky "art form", who cooked you dinners and watched The Graduate with you cuddled up on the sofa and was your own secret Mrs Robinson, only much nicer. Doesn't all that count for anything any more?' But, with a twinge of regret, I determined not to contact him again.

Crispin had texted several times after our one-night stand, using various enticements (e.g. cooking me an Oriental meal) to tempt me into further romps. But I always demurred, at times with a touch of self-irony:

Me: Crispin, I like you but I'm the wrong person for you. You should stick to your own generation. Have a proper relationship, as opposed to a sex match. You need a real long-term partner. Don't be deflected by the likes of me.

Crispin: Ah, the most gentle of let-downs. But I'd love to be wrong with you one more night. Keep my number and if you ever want some no-strings fun please call me.

But I was becoming a tad jaded with no-strings fun, which could just as easily turn out to be no-strings no-fun.

Erik had kept in touch too, with plenty of lols and smiley faces, but receiving scant encouragement from me, his messages eventually petered out. Even Bob had stopped threatening to 'seduce' me over that much-vaunted but never materialising dinner.

Then there was Elliot, the handsome, sporty teacher. I wasn't bothered about seeing him again but it really annoyed me that he wasn't bothered about seeing me, either. He never even asked me out on a second date. What was wrong with him? Was it another case of *je ne sais quoi*? I refused to brood on the notion that there might be something wrong with *me*. The Raven? Single, sexy and sixty-one? Impossible! Elliot was churlish, that's all. Or blind. Maybe both.

But my feeling that night that something was not right wasn't due to this catalogue of dating damp squibs. It came from the realisation that I didn't actually care about any of these men. Not in any deeply meaningful way. I wanted to. I wanted, in particular, to care about Pup. And of course I did. But it seemed easy enough to let him go and I wondered why it wasn't harder.

Delete, delete, delete. I erased them all. Had all these human beings, even the good and likeable ones, become mere off-the-shelf products to me and dispensable in our throw-away society? I didn't want to feel like that.

But I suspected I might feel like that for some time. And

it would only be when I crossed paths with someone who was genuinely special to me, and for whom I was special, that I could learn to care more profoundly again. And perhaps that day would never come.

At our last chinwag, Sara had reiterated: 'You know you need to stop seeing these young guys, right? You can't keep having horny twenty-something strangers turning up at all hours. You should look for a real relationship with a decent man your own age.'

'Where do I find one of those?'

'Dating sites for seniors.' She'd given me a cautious look, knowing that the very word 'senior' would make me shudder.

'No thanks.'

However, a certain shameful notion did, from time to time, pop up in some dark crevice of my mind and I knew I'd be hauled over the coals for it by the feminist sisterhood. Proudly independent though I was, and self-reliant and liberated and all those fine things, I reasoned that if some worthy bloke with a modest fortune came along who thought the sun beamed out of my orifices and offered to look after me forever, whisk me off on exotic holidays and put my grandsons through Eton, I'd be a fool not to leap at the chance. And it wouldn't matter if he looked more like Stanley Tucci than Pierce Brosnan, as long as he wasn't desperately boring. Mildly boring I could handle.

The next time I saw Vanessa in the pool she informed me that it was all over between her and Gerald. The relationship had lasted less than a month. He had been generous to a fault. Kind. Looked after all her needs. Great in bed (she said that twice for added emphasis).

'So what was wrong?' I asked.

She reflected for a moment, as she idly did a few warm-up swirls with her arms. 'Hard to put my finger on it. I just knew I couldn't carry on spending my time with him. At the end of the day he was just too, you know…'

'Too normal?'

'Yeah. Way too normal.'

'Not enough personality, no oomph?'

'Exactly. I like a man who can bring something to the table. Besides a bottle of wine.'

Apparently they had spent the weekend together and things went well enough until the Sunday evening, when they were chilling out at her place and he offered to cook dinner. 'And he was so *nice* every time he wanted to use something in my kitchen. He kept asking whether he could use this knife and that saucepan, and whether I minded him using the oregano, or would I prefer the thyme, and I wished he wouldn't be so bloody *nice*. I wanted him to be a proper man, stop asking my permission and just *do it*.'

'Yeah,' I said. 'It's terrible when they're so nice. Making you dinner and all that.'

'So I kicked him out later that night. It was about 2 a.m. And I'm sorry that I hurt him but it couldn't be helped. I wouldn't let him sleep over, not even on the sofa. I said he could get a cab home.'

'Where does he live?'

'Surrey.'

'Bloody hell, that would have cost him over a hundred quid. But I guess he's rich, right?'

'Well, it turns out he's not even that rich,' Vanessa said nonchalantly as she plopped onto her back with a splash. I could tell she was no longer interested in discussing Gerald.

The only positive thing about the Gerald debacle was that now Vanessa would be renewing her membership on the dating site. I'm not sure why (sensing as I did that I might not be on the site much longer myself) but I found this thought comforting.

I was surprised to receive a text out of the blue from tattooed Tinder boy Damian, who had been due to come over a couple of months earlier but blew me out with some lame excuse involving overtime work and traffic jams. 'Hey, sexy. How are you?' He said he was up for arranging a get-together, if I gave him another chance.

Well, I was having a quiet week and could still picture his hunky illustrated torso and cute, roguish grin. Besides, I've always found it hard to maintain a grudge. So I decided to give him the benefit of the doubt and said sure, let's do it. At which he stoked up the proceedings with a few graphic messages about our likely activities, the bawdy devil.

We agreed on a rendezvous, a few days away. Once again he said he would drive over from his workplace outside London and arrive at my house early in the evening, with plenty of time for fun and frolics. I was definitely ready for this and the prospect charged me with frissons of anticipation. I wondered whether I should wear a silk dress, out of which I could slip gracefully at *le bon moment* or tight trousers to emphasise my hard-earned rear. All-important decisions.

In the event my sartorial deliberations were irrelevant.

Because, for a second time, the much-vaunted assignation never took place. I texted him on the morning of the big day to confirm arrangements, then again in the afternoon. But when no reply came I realised he would be a no-show. I would have been furious with him, as well as with myself for giving him the opportunity once again to take me for a fool, except that, mercifully, I didn't care all that much. Perhaps he had a wife and kids, perhaps he was a pathetic fantasist, what did it matter? I decided to send him one last text: 'I don't care what your dodgy bullshit is. You'll never hear from me again.'

Instead of an evening of rampant sex, I flopped down on the sofa and watched the latest episode of Downton Abbey with a glass of red wine and bowl of olives, and was perfectly content. Is that Tom Branson hot or what?

A few days later my mobile rang and an unknown number came up. It was a woman with a south London accent who apologised for disturbing me, then said she was calling because she had found texts from me on her boyfriend's mobile and feared he had been cheating on her. She needed to know what was going on; was I having an affair with him?

Fuck, fuck, fuck, I thought, *here we go. Which one of those bastards is it*? I had already forgotten about my recently aborted tryst with Damian. But a moment later it became clear that it was indeed the tattooed would-be lothario. This explained his erratic behaviour and came as no surprise to me, as I had imagined something of the sort. He was another Rajesh, except that he wasn't upfront about being 'in a relationship'. I honestly didn't know which cheat's tactic was worse.

Apparently Damian's girlfriend grew suspicious, examined

his phone and confronted him about my messages (how embarrassing), whereupon he admitted that we had met via Tinder. But then he told her that she needn't worry about me because I was sixty. What a bloody nerve! As if we sexagenarians couldn't cause as much worry as anyone else.

She said she was in her early thirties, the same age as him, and they had been together 'a very long time'. She sounded desperate and I felt sorry for the girl.

'Listen,' I told her, 'we never met in person. It didn't go any further than texting.'

I could hear the relief in her voice. 'So at least he didn't lie about that, anyway.'

'No, but a guy with a girlfriend shouldn't be on Tinder in the first place, looking for sex partners. And he's got all these hard-core fantasies about older women. They're not going to go away soon. I don't think you can trust him.'

'I know,' she said. 'I've felt that for a long while.' She paused and sighed. 'I'm glad I called you. Thanks for being honest with me. Men like that are losers. Don't realise what they have till it's gone.'

'Dump him.'

'Yeah, I will. Everything happens for a reason, so I guess it's good this happened. I know I really need to move on. I deserve better than this.'

'Of course you do.'

'Only problem is, I work with him. So I'll have to keep seeing him around.'

'Oh, what a bummer.'

We spoke a while longer, then wished each other good luck for the future and said good-bye.

I reflected on how easy it was to view each 'match' acquired on a dating site or app entirely within the context of its own little self-contained digital existence, to forget that that same man was also living a whole other life in the real world, a complicated life that you knew nothing about, alongside people you knew nothing about. This was the first time that one of those unknown correlated people had reached across and dipped into my own real-world life. And that had a certain shock value.

I regretted the part I had unwittingly played in this woman's pain. On the other hand, perhaps I had done her a favour. In any case I wanted to give her a final few words of encouragement. So before putting the unfortunate episode behind me forever I sent her a text.

'Be strong. Back in the seventies my generation fought for women's independence. Make the most of it!'

Admittedly I didn't do any of that fighting myself, because I always had other things on my mind besides marching around with banners. But she didn't need to know that.

CHAPTER TWENTY-ONE

There could have been all manner of neat Hollywood endings to this book. A particularly fine one would have been for Charles to turn up at my door one day and sweep me into his arms, having resolved his onerous issues, declare that I was The One for him because I was cute and funny and sexy and could converse on so many absorbing topics, and promise that we would never again be too busy for wonderful little me. Good-bye to all the other online contestants, they can carry on a-winkin' all they like, it would be to no avail!

And after this affirmation of love, Charles carries me upstairs to the bedroom (the way Clark Gable carried Vivien Leigh in Gone with the Wind), and in the course of some fabulous sex which goes on *for hours* I get my long-lost orgasm back and the next thing you know it's ding dong the bells are gonna chime.

But you always knew it wouldn't end that way. Because this is not a romcom with Meryl Streep and Steve Martin. This is real life we've been talking about here, which is even more 'complicated'.

So I'll tell you the way it really ends. Faithful readers, you've stayed with me this far. Now try to imagine the most ghastly calamity that could befall the Raven, the most awful, gut-wrenching, worst case scenario (after being kidnapped by the Taliban, obviously). Yes, that's *exactly* what happened.

One morning, in one instant, with the arrival on my laptop of a single email, my grand project was brought to a juddering halt. The email was from my long-departed ex-partner, who announced that he would be moving back in with me. Yes, without so much as a by-your-leave, he would be returning to what was once our home but was now *my* home, thereby wrecking my proud new independence.

His return was not due to the sudden realisation that he had made a terrible mistake by buggering off, and couldn't live without me. This was no mea culpa. No, the decision was taken 'regrettably' for purely financial reasons.

My immediate reaction was disbelief, quickly followed by anger, because my ex wasn't given to making bad jokes (or good ones) and I knew it was no idle threat. A year and a half after he had moved out of our jointly owned house into rented accommodation, our property was still on the market. This was bad news all round, but obviously worse for him. I understood the financial imperatives and had some sympathy for his situation. On the other hand, leaving had been his choice, not mine. When he left it took me months to get my equilibrium back – months of hurt and loneliness and distress. But as you have doubtless gathered over the course of these many chapters, I was now comfortable in my skin, cherishing my freedom and proud of my autonomy. I had rather taken to this whole splendid isolation gig. And the prospect of having to share my personal space once more with the ex who had dumped me, of having him know my business, and who my business was with, was odious in the extreme. In my new incarnation I was retro-spectively overjoyed that I had been ditched, and didn't want to be un-ditched, not even for purely financial reasons.

When I explained this turn of events to Vanessa she was outraged on my behalf and proposed a typically uncompro-mising solution to the problem: 'You need to get a doctor's certificate saying that being forced to live with him again will be so stressful that you'll have a nervous breakdown and be unable to earn your living. That should do the trick!'

But it wasn't true. And anyway, I didn't hate my ex that much. I didn't hate him at all. I just didn't want him around, dragging me backwards with his presence and its echoes of the past. So I appealed to him to choose some other solution.

Solution One: he could move in with his girlfriend. (Sorry, didn't I mention he had a girlfriend?) But he claimed her place was too small.

Solution Two: he could live with his father for a while. His place was big enough. But no, the ex countered that his extremely aged father lived outside London, was too infirm and would be overly demanding. No lies there.

Solution Three: I could let out the empty bedrooms to lodgers and give him all the money so that he could continue renting a place for himself. But even I realised this would not solve my problem. I'd have as much privacy living with lodgers as I would have living with him. And at least with him I'd be able to manipulate his feelings of guilt to my advantage…

In the end, after much fuming to myself, I realised I could do nothing to forestall this outcome. I could only pray that we wouldn't have to co-exist for very long, that we would be able to shift the property soon, so that we could each take our share of the dosh and run.

It was apparent to me that as well as generally cramping my style, big time, this unwanted new domestic arrangement would put the kibosh on my days of dating dangerously.

I mused on how things might play out. Let's see.

Scrumptious and biddable young man on our first date accompanies me home late at night and asks: 'Who's that guy in the kitchen making himself a cup of tea?' Whereupon I smile sweetly and consider lying. My lodger? A cousin visiting from abroad? A house-mate? I opt for the truth, on the basis that he is bound to find out at some point anyway. 'That's my ex.' At this unexpected response the young man looks startled and confused, is no longer biddable, and mumbles something which sounds like 'Weird. I'm outta here.' Desperately I call after his retreating back: 'Wait! It's okay! We live together for purely financial reasons!' But it's too late. My hunk, who had promised so much, has disappeared into the night, never to return.

Yep, that sounds about right.

I always understood that part of my appeal to young men, who generally lived with flatmates or their families, was that I lived on my own. I was an independent older woman with a house to herself, total privacy, no one else around to see anything or interfere or create inhibiting factors. But that would no longer be the case.

Perhaps I could get away with a little ducking and diving, like a character in an Alan Ayckbourn bedroom farce. Doors opening and closing in the middle of the night, comic misunderstandings, naked buttocks hurrying down hallways...But

I didn't have the stomach for all that. It sounded too tiring. Maybe I was just too old for it.

I also had no need of my ex's shock, disapproval, concern and discomfiture – all of which would come my way in great heaps once he got wind of the racy goings-on in our co-habited house. No, my two dating site memberships were due to expire soon anyway, so I reckoned it was easier to call it a day. Perhaps only temporarily. I couldn't be sure. I had long stopped trying to predict the future, and this Raven, unlike Poe's original, never says Nevermore.

As the day of my ex's return neared, I began to mourn the approaching loss of my liberty. It had taken me to the age of sixty to discover what it was like to live alone. A late baptism of fire, which had at first burned me painfully but which now lit and warmed my world. That solitary life was about far more for me than the freedom to bang boys. It was about the freedom, at last, to be myself, wherever that took me, and lately it had taken me down some shadowy and chancy, not always wholesome but always thoroughly invigorating rabbit holes. My adventures in dating-land. They had been the perfect counterpoint to the other side of me, the side which comprised the softness and unsparing love which I had for my children and grandchildren. No matriarch was more devoted to her family than me.

Matriarch, Raven. Two vastly different roles but I tackled both with gusto, at full throttle. No holding back, no lame-ass half-measures. Isn't that the way to take on any role in life?

*

It was less than a fortnight before my ex was due to move back in, when I got an unexpected text one afternoon from my erstwhile Tinder boy, Jake. It had been two months since we last had contact, on that surreal night when a sloshed Bob fell into my pond whilst I was replying to the brawny young 'un's booty call. Now he was thrillingly on my case again with 'Hi, sexy. How are you?'

'Hello, baby. I'm good. But then you already knew that!'

'Ha ha, yes I did, and you are! What are you up to tonight?'

I wasn't up to anything. And if I had been, I would gladly have un-upped myself to it in favour of a roll in the hay with Jake. After all, the window of opportunity for this pastime would not remain open for long. Which called to my mind the words of Badfinger's evergreen hit song of four decades earlier:

Sonny, if you want it, here it is, come and get it. But you better hurry 'cause it's going fast.

'Come on over, Jake,' I texted back. 'I'd love to see you. xxx'

'Great…will be there at 8. xxx'

I felt my insides stirring. My world was once more aburst with flashing fairy lights. I tossed my mobile onto the bed and put on my CD of Cher's greatest hits – at full belter volume, of course – then ran myself a warm, fragrant bath. And do you know, as I luxuriated amidst the bubbles, eyes closed, picturing the rampant romps to come, it was as if the diva of divas were right there with me.

So there you have it. My racy dating memoir. Anyway that's what I thought it was, until a publisher I met referred to it as a 'sex memoir', a category of book I had never even heard of before, innocent creature that I am. Sex memoir? Well fair enough, there is plenty of sex in it, although it delves into other aspects of human life too – love and relationships, desire and disappointment, ageing and the generation gap. But if I've written a sex memoir, so be it. No big deal. My goodness, sex is everywhere these days in our 21st century Western world. And often in far more explicit and base forms than anything contained in my little tome. Who could possibly object to the Raven's carefree frolics?

Ha! I know better now. Despite our progressive 'anything goes' society – in which gay couples can marry and raise children, transgender folk can swap sexes to suit, and reconstituted families can set up households in any configuration they like – the concept of an older woman enjoying intimacy with a much younger man is a lifestyle choice which still shocks many people. I didn't think there was much sap left in the 'Disgusted of Tunbridge Wells' brigade but boy, did I ever get that wrong.

My book burst on to the public consciousness overnight via a three-part serialisation in a major British tabloid paper. And it would be an understatement to say that my life has not been the same since. That tabloid has the most popular newspaper website in the world, read by 50 million people, and as I was to discover, quite a few of them did not approve of me and my book.

I have been a journalist all my working life and am no stranger to controversy, having written various first-person pieces which have divided public opinion. But that was before the rise of the human sub-species known as the internet troll. Once that lot got their anonymous mitts on my story they subjected me to a volley of vitriol and I admit I felt hurt. But not for long. First of all I simply stopped reading their inane comments, which was surprisingly easy to do. And secondly, if you have worked as a feature writer at the bad-ass *Daily Mail,* as I did throughout most of the 1990s, you will have acquired survival mechanisms in the face of human harshness: otherwise known as a thick skin.

Still, for the first week or two I reeled from the glare of attention directed at me from around the globe, both negative and positive. Because of course there was a lot of favourable feedback too. At first this came mainly from men. Yes, I was a big hit with the male readers of my story. As it was picked up by the media in country after country, I started receiving messages from them – young men and older men, Turkish men with unpronounceable names and broken English, jovial Aussies, formal-sounding Indians, Irish charmers, a whole slew of suave Mediterranean types, and so on.

Except for two or three cases, the senders of these messages were very well-behaved. They generally said the same thing: they think I'm 'beautiful', they admire me, they would be privileged if one day they could meet me. It all made me sound like a cross between Marilyn Monroe and Mother Theresa. But just as I had felt the opprobrium to be way over-the-top, this adulation struck me as somewhat excessive.

Suddenly the whole world seemed to know my name and my story, which made me feel metaphorically naked, and I guess that is one definition of 'fame'. Overnight my pool of Facebook friends grew from 350 to nearly 1000. And these new fans all wanted to chat with me online. Well, I couldn't keep that little lark up for long.

What I found even more encouraging were the warmly supportive emails from other women of my generation. For example this, from a woman called Anna:

Like you, I am 61 and been told I don't look, feel or act my age. No elasticated skirts or sensible shoes for me... yet! Like you, I joined a dating site, lied about my age by four years and yes, I have been approached by much younger men too. Only thing is, I have never pursued it, due to lack of confidence. I envy and admire your outlook to life in the 60s and all I can say is... good for you. I hope you make shedloads with your book and then stick two fingers up at the "haters". I am looking forward to reading about your adventures and probably wishing it was me. Take care, continue having fun and there might be another book out when you're in your 70s.

After my appearance on the popular ITV breakfast show This Morning, women wrote to me in greater numbers. I was in the cab on my way home, having just left the TV studio, when their messages started pinging on to my mobile.

From Lucy (sent from her iPhone):

I've just watched your interview on This Morning, *you are giving women the confidence.*

And from Angela:

The criticism of your book is due to a lack of knowledge, as loads of women are doing this! Am 44 and been having loads of unstrung sex with guys 25 and up... I do not envisage this stopping unless I meet my Mr Right. The sex as echoed in your book extracts is dangerous but fun and I feel great.

That day was a turning point for me as I realised that I really had become a kind of role model for older women. Not by any means the first or the only one to indulge in bedroom delights with younger men, but the first to be so unabashed about it, to write about it with total candour, not as anything kinky or outlandish but as a simple fact of life. And I could see that that meant something.

With some women, however, there was a distinct lack of sisterly sympathy, and I'm not referring merely to those indelicate female trolls online. There was the 55-year-old tabloid columnist who berated me for my behaviour, of which she heartily disapproved, like some po-faced Victorian prude... but only after informing readers that she herself received plenty of come-ons from young men, all of which she nobly rejected. Yes dear, we believe you.

And there was the forty-something book reviewer, married with young kids, who completely misunderstood my motives, believing my wild escapades to have been a sad attempt to stave off loneliness. Wrong! Far from being sad and lonely at that point in my life, I was relishing my new freedom and independence. I did what I did in order to pack in the adventure while the going was good. I went looking for fun and excitement. And I found it.

That said, as my story hit the headlines over and over again (and what scandalous headlines they were, e.g. 'The Grandmother Who Dated 20-Year-Old Men - And Loved It!') and even some of my friends were stunned into silence, and my family wasn't exactly relishing the media spotlight, I did have the odd *mea culpa* moment. I would stop, hold my head in my hands and ask myself: what on earth have I unleashed? This book will follow me everywhere. Whatever else I have written or will write, I will always be the woman who 'put the sex into sexagenarian'. And at moments like that I considered my response, should someone ask whether, in view of the furore kicked up by Raven, the controversy and the scorching criticism, I would still have written the book as I did. Would I still publish and be damned?

Bloody right I would.